MW00849147

SAQI ESSENTIALS

Timeless, engaging and informative, Saqi Essentials are reference works that have attained the status of true classics on the Middle East. They represent milestones in scholarly writing, ranging across history, politics, sociology, gender studies and philosophy, aimed at both the specialist and general reader.

ADONIS

# Sufism & Surrealism

*Translated from the Arabic by*
Judith Cumberbatch

**SAQI**

First English language edition published 2005 by Saqi Books
This edition published 2016

First published in Arabic as *al-Sufiyya wal Surriyaliyya*
by Dar al Saqi, Beirut, 1995

Copyright © Adonis, 2005
Translation copyright © Judith Cumberbatch, 2005

Adonis has asserted his right under the Copyright, Designs
and Patents Act, 1988, to be identified as the author of this work.

This book is sold subject to the condition that it shall not, by way of trade
or otherwise, be lent, resold, hired out, or otherwise circulated without the
publisher's prior consent in any form of binding or cover other than that in
which it is published and without a similar condition including this
condition being imposed on the subsequent purchaser.

ISBN 978-0-86356-189-4
eISBN 978-0-86356-712-4

A full CIP record for this book is available from the British Library.

Printed and bound by CPI Group (UK) Ltd, Croydon, CR0 4YY

Saqi Books
26 Westbourne Grove
London W2 5RH
www.saqibooks.com

# Contents

# Introduction

1

Sufism and Surrealism is a title that will arouse controversy if not disgust among those interested in Surrealism, as well as Sufism. It would be surprising to find a consensus, whether this interest is positive or negative.

The prime objection that will be raised will be that Sufism is a religious movement, oriented towards religious salvation, whereas Surrealism is an atheistic movement, with no aspirations to heavenly salvation. Is it possible to link the religious and the secular? Although such an objection appears valid, it does not completely rule out the possibility that many of the intellectual issues inherent in Sufism and Surrealism are similar to or intersect with each other. Atheism does not necessarily exclude mysticism, nor does Sufism necessarily include a belief in traditional religion or a traditional belief in religion.

In any case, this objection is of fundamental benefit to the researcher as it compels him to cast a fresh eye on the accepted meaning and definition of both Surrealism and Sufism and to understand them in a new way. It is true to say that God, in the traditional religious sense of the word, does not exist in Surrealism, as André Breton confirms when he says that the sacred in which he believes is either not religious or is outside religion. But it is also true to say that God, in the traditional religious sense of the word, is not present in Sufism, or, rather, let us say that in Sufism God does not have a separate and distinct existence from the created universe as he does in orthodox religion, but is a part of it, a presence of unity and oneness. God in Sufism is not only the one but also the many. He is part of existence, the high point (as Breton calls it), the point at which what we call matter and what we call the spirit come together and all contradictions between the two are eliminated. He is not only the one who has brought the created universe into being, as an external being and without being joined to it, but he is also the created universe itself in its dynamism and infinity. He is not in the sky or on earth, but is the sky and earth together merged into one. Journeying to him does not demand that we leave existence and ourselves, but instead that we go further and further into existence and ourselves. The infinite (God) is not outside matter; it is in matter. The infinite is man and matter. He is somewhere or other but inside the place as well. He is another country, but it exists about us and in us.

When talking about Sufism, therefore, we have to abandon prevailing doctrines and orthodox interpretations in particular.

We have to go back to its origins. From the very beginning, Sufi doctrines were linked to what was hidden and transcendental. The movement towards Sufism came about because reason, religious orthodoxy and science were unable to answer many of the profound questions posed by man. For man felt that there were problems that continued to disturb him even when all intellectual, religious, legal and scientific problems had been solved by logical, legal and scientific means. This is what was insoluble (is insoluble), was unknown (is unknown), was not spoken about (is not spoken about). It is what gave birth to Sufism. It was these same factors that led to the emergence of Surrealism. Surrealism claimed primarily to be a movement, which spoke what had not been nor was spoken about. The essence of Sufism, as I understand it was the unspoken, the unseen, the unknown.

The ultimate goal of the Sufi is to become one with the invisible, that is, the absolute. The Surrealist aspires to the same thing; the nature of the absolute – be it God, reason, matter itself, thought or spirit – or rather the motion of becoming absorbed into it is unimportant, as is the path that leads to it. In all cases there is a return to the origin of creation, whatever that origin is. It is a return that assumes an alteration in the one who is at the same time returning to and merging with the origin. The origin, in other words, remains itself as it is revealed through its creations and as its creations return to it.

# 2

In an article by Guy-René Doumayrou,[1] the writer quickly distinguishes between Surrealism and esotericism, saying that the former is a movement that seeks enlightenment from an invisible light, the light (of the spirit?) or thought, and which seeks to uncover the true action of this thought, whereas the second tries to uncover the hidden functions of nature. While Surrealism strives to 'return freedom to thought', esotericism works to free the spirit. He says that the 'supreme point' to which Breton refers is not mysticism and cites what Breton says in one of his 'Entretiens':

> It is well known that the point at which we can resolve all the contradictions which gnaw away at us and create despair, and which, in my book *Amour fou*, I have termed 'the supreme point', remembering a beautiful spot in the lower Alps, cannot be attained through mysticism.[2]

Judging by the article and the context in which the word is used, it is most likely that the word 'mysticism' here means esotericism.

Doumayrou says that since its inception, Surrealism has constantly been amazed by the spontaneous images that flow out from dreams and through the use of oral and creative tools and the systematic activities it practises, which reached their peak with

Robert Desnos, who was able to sleep at will even in the rowdy atmosphere of a café. The poet Aragon described these activities as 'an extraordinary experiment. Despite psychoanalysis, we could almost explain them metaphysically.'[3]

The writer (Doumayrou) states that the Surrealists, individually and collectively, are constantly preoccupied with finding ways of expressing 'the true functioning of thought' through 'psychic tools', outside any control exercised by reason or any aesthetic or moral concern, and of releasing the unconscious in the channels of daily life.

He says subsequently that Surrealism is profoundly interested in the irrational but not to the extent of believing in a God or divine power, as Michel Carrouges and Pierre Klossowski try to claim (p. 3 of Doumayrou's article). The Surrealists believe that any distinction between the imaginative and the real is meaningless. Reality as they understand it is not the reality of the common illusions of dualism. Imagination, they believe, is what guides the conscious to the nub of agitation or the 'vibrations fondatrices' (ibid., p. 4). The issue in fact concerns a world of vibrations, according to Doumayrou, which specialist writers continue to affirm when speaking about auras.

Some writers assert that everyone is surrounded by three levels of vibrations – colour, extensity and sense. But 'if we are to believe Carlos Castaneda and his Yaqui shaman, seeing these things in a way other than by chance demands a very harsh training' (ibid., p. 5).

The author points to what Breton says about the link between Surrealism and nature, in which he asserts that, 'the Surrealists find it difficult to accept the premise that nature is the enemy of man, but rather assume that man has lost the keys to it, which he possesses intuitively and which used to keep him in intimate and constant contact with it.' Since that time he has been trying other keys in vain (ibid., p. 5; Entretiens, p. 248).

Breton goes on to say that, 'There is no value in a scientific knowledge of nature unless there is contact with nature through poetic and, dare I say, mythic ways' (Entretiens, p. 248).

Finally, the writer recognizes that the esoteric dimension (internal, hidden) and the knowledge of magic and the occult appear in the second Surrealist manifesto to explain the general human crisis

(Doumayrou article, p. 6) when Breton points to the similarities between what the Surrealists and Alchemists are searching for. 'Surrealist research', he says, 'along with alchemic research presents a remarkable unity of purpose. The philosopher's stone is nothing other than a thing, which should be given to man's imagination to take forcible revenge on everything, and after years of taming the spirit and crazy submission, here we are again, attempting finally to free this imagination by the long, huge, reasoned deregulation of the senses' (*Second Manifesto*, 1930, see article pp. 6–7).

3

I have spent a long time on this article because it is the most recent to discuss the relationship between Surrealism and the abstract or hidden world. Whether it is viewed negatively or positively, nevertheless everything in it points to the depth of this relationship and its fundamental importance, as long as the traditional religious dimension is excluded from the abstract and hidden. Sufism, as I understand it, and as I will seek to show, is definitely not without such a dimension and does not oppose it, particularly from an intellectual viewpoint. However, I believe that such objections as I pointed to at the beginning will continue to be raised. Surrealism, for example, is regarded as an artistic and cultural movement, with poetry, prose and plastic arts, while Sufism is seen as a religious movement, whose output can be studied only in documents that explain its ideas and religious beliefs. In addition, there do not appear to be any linguistic or historical ties linking the two, although this can be explained by the paucity of critical work on Sufism and the poor understanding of it, which in general demonstrates the low level of theoretical knowledge of those who study Arab culture and the wretched picture they present of the culture itself.

However, I hasten to add that the intention of this research is not to say that Sufism is the same as Surrealism or that Sufism has had a direct or indirect influence on Surrealism because it has been longer established. The intention is, rather, to confirm that an interior world exists, which is invisible, unknown and inaccessible by logical or rational means. Without it, and without attempting to attain it, people are incomplete beings who lack existence and knowledge. The ways to it are particular and specific. This is evidenced by the kinship and harmony that exists between all those groups that seek to penetrate the unseen and which specifically include the Sufis and the Surrealists. Important attempts at knowing the hidden side of being intersect in one form or another, in ways that are beyond language, time and culture. I will attempt to portray this encounter between Sufism and Surrealism and to explain that both of them have followed the same path to knowledge, although they have different names and follow different goals. The similarities that exist allow one to say that Surrealism is a pagan form of Sufism whose goal is to become one with the absolute, whereas Sufism is Surrealist in that it searches for the Absolute and seeks to immerse itself in it.

Yes, at certain moments, man feels that he needs something other than the book (revelation) or reason or knowledge to speak to him. A tree, a stone, a mountain or stream.

At such moments, man feels that ideas exist not only in his head but in his entire body and at one time or another might be more present in his feet than in his head. He feels the idea as a profound union between two bodies rather than two thoughts and, rather than speak to another human being, he feels the need to become one with, for example, a wave.

At this moment, he becomes aware that truth does not come from books or revelation or laws or ideas or science but from an interior world, from living experience, from love and from the continuing vital interconnection between things and the universe. It becomes clear that man constantly longs to embody and to be embodied, rather than to separate or be separate. He thirsts for union rather than obscurity, for participation rather than hegemony. He is convinced that if God exists, as a separate being outside the created universe and linked to it by nothing more than the fact of creation and rule, then the world is nothing but a ball of dust and does not deserve to exist or, to put it more explicitly, does not deserve that man (that great being) should live on it. The creature will be more important than its creator. If there is nothing more to existence than heaven or hell, then it obviously becomes a competition, and a silly competition at that, risible and unworthy of mankind.

At such moments man becomes increasingly aware that in the depths of his being there is a mighty ocean, which is walled and reined in by obstacles and dams of every description. If he does not plunge into it and break down the dams and walls (which are holding back the water) to see what he has not seen (what is not seen) and think about what has not been thought about and feel something that no one believes can be attained, then his life will be like foam on the crest of a wave. If he submerges himself in this ocean, a world will open up to him that is unlimited by things and whose only boundaries are thought and imagination. It has no limits, except those imposed by thought and imagination.

Perhaps this moment is the true moment of love. In love, man and woman emerge from their individual selves and become one, in a form of unity in which they believe they mean more together than they do separately. Together they are real and absolute, existing and transcendental. The one becomes the other. He/she is manifest in the other as part of, above, with and like the other.

This moment is definitely the point at which Sufism and Surrealism meet.

4

Ibn Taymiyya pronounced the following *fatwah* on Sufism: 'The nature of these people is evil, as they contradict the messengers (prayers and the peace of God be upon them), as is apparent from the words of the writer of the *Futuhat al-Makiyya*, the *Fusus* and other writings. He praises unbelievers such as the tribe of Noah and

Hud and Pharaoh and others like them and disagrees with prophets such as Noah and Ibrahim and Moses and Haroun; he censures the sheikhs of Islam, who are praised by the Muslims, such as Junaid bin Muhammad and Sahel bin Abd Allah al-Testari and praises those who are censured by the Muslims, such as al-Hallaj and his like, just as he mentions him in his satanic revelations' (al-Fatawah 11/239, Riyadh 1382 AH).

I tend towards the belief that this is a sound *fatwah* from the point of view of Ibn Taymiyya, i.e. from the point of view of a literal and orthodox understanding of the text of the Qur'an. It is not possible to find a clear source for the Sufi vision; it does not appear in the text of the Qur'an, as the first Muslims understood it, nor in the sayings of the Prophet, if they are interpreted literally and in an orthodox manner according to classical tradition. In fact, the opposite is true; there is nothing in Sufism that overtly disagrees with the issue of the creator or creation as it appears in the religious texts.

However, Sufism understands the religious texts and explains them in a radically different way from that adopted by the literal and canonical school. It regards the Prophet himself, in speech and in deed, as a model of Sufism, but that is another matter.

Perhaps we should look at how Ibn Taymiyya, an exemplar of the orthodox view, understands Sufism. He divides it into two categories: the specific and the absolute. As for the specific, he says, 'the Christians say, as do the al-Ghalia of the Rafidun about the imams and the ignorant poor and Sufis about the sheikhs, that unity can mean the unity of water and yoghurt, or *hulul* (becoming one with), or unity of one kind or another.'

As for absolute *hulul* (pantheism), this means that God the most high is, in essence, present in everything and this is what the Sunni and the Salaf say about those who lived in the dark ages.

And what they (the Sufis) say about general unity has been said, as far as I know, only by those who deny the creator, like the Pharaoh of the Carmathians. For in reality, they believe that the essence of the existence of God is the essence of the existence of creation, and the existence of the essence of God, the creator of heaven and earth, is the same as what has been created. They don't imagine that God created others or that he is the lord of two worlds, or he is rich while others are poor. Such people can be divided into three factions:

> The first branch believes that all essences, the essences of animals, plants and minerals, movements and non-movements are fixed in non-being, which is eternal and everlasting, and the existence of truth (God) flows over these essences and their existence is the existence of God, but their essences are not the essence of God. This faction distinguishes between existence and immutability. When you are immutable, you will appear in your existence.
>
> As for the second faction, they believe that the existence of what has been created is the exact existence of the creator and it is not different from or other than it.
>
> As for the third faction, they believe that there is no other in any other form, and that man sees the other only when he is covered by a veil. When the veil is lifted from his face, he sees there is no one else and the matter becomes clear to him.

Ibn Taymiyya believes that the heretical nature of Sufism lies in the fact that they prefer their opinion to the revealed word of God (the Book). 'They prefer to follow their desires rather than God's orders, so they give themselves up to experience and ecstatic ardour and such things because they love and desire such worship.' He regards this as the origin of all sins committed by sinners.[4] Desire is fancy, lust and instant gratification.[5] Thus, as Ibn Taymiyya sees it, these people's love of 'listening to poems, songs and musical instruments, which rouse absolute love, is not the preserve of the believers alone, but is shared by those who love God, idolaters, lovers of the cross, lovers of brothers and young men and women. Such people follow their senses and their passions without respecting the Qur'an or the Sunna or the path the Salaf of the Umma followed.'[6] In other words, Sufism is worshipping God without following orders or laws, and worshipping him with 'desire, fancies and heresies'. This is what happens to the Sufis when they do something abnormal or demand that their prayers be answered, which are against the accepted norm. There is one way for them to escape from the loss facing them and that is to 'obey God's command' and 'adhere to Sunni tradition', for the Sunni path, as Malik says, is 'like Noah's ark. Those who sail in it will be saved, and those who fail to board it will drown.'[7]

In another letter, Ibn Taymiyya says that the Sufis 'base their beliefs on desire, and desire is necessary as long as it is the desire to worship God alone in the way he ordered.'[8] He continues, 'The theologians base their beliefs on an exigent view of knowledge and this is also necessary on condition that one is knowledgeable about what the Prophet told us and that one looks at the proofs, which the Prophet showed us, the marvels of God ... Those who seek knowledge without desire or desire without knowledge are lost and those who seek this without following what the Prophet said about them are also lost.' He concludes by saying that Islam revolves around two principles – 'the worship of one God and the worship of him according to his laws and not through innovation or heresy.'[9]

Ibn Taymiyya's *fatwah* on Sufism brings to mind the manner in which Surrealism was first received. People in cultural circles looked upon it with amazement and ridicule, and called anything surreal that broke with traditional aestheticism.[10]

The Sufi Ahmed bin Muhammad bin Ajiba al-Hassani, in contrast to Ibn Taymiyya, speaks about the origins of Sufism as follows: 'Its subject is the divine essence of God, because the Sufi searches for him in order to know him, either through signs or witnessing him or seeing him with his own eyes. The first applies to those who are seeking [God/knowledge] (*al-Talibuna*) and the second to those who have attained it (*al-Wasiluna*). The founder of the science of Sufism is the Prophet himself (prayers and peace be upon him), who learnt it from God through revelation and inspiration. Gibril, may peace be upon him, first descended and brought the *shari'a* (God's law), and then, when it was established, he descended to the earth again with the truth, a chosen part of it, rather than its entirety. The first person to speak about Sufism and demonstrate it was Our Lord Ali (God's grace be upon him)' (*al-Futuhat al-Ilahiya fi Sharh al-Mabahith al-Asliya*, p. 5).

He distinguishes between the *shari'a*, the *tariqa* and the *haqiqa* as follows: '*shari'a* is the worship of God, *tariqa* is the search for God and *haqiqa* is the sight of God' (ibid., p. 38).

Ibn Ajiba sees man as 'the divine model'. God has given him his spiritual attributes, so 'man's true nature and his secrets come from the secrets of God. When they are written about, they should not be referred to directly, but only mentioned indirectly and in code' (ibid., pp. 41–43). The secret of 'divinity, which God has placed in man, cannot be perfectly understood by anyone except God himself' (ibid., pp. 46–47).

Ibn Ajiba addresses man as follows: 'The knowledge of spiritual experience cannot be obtained from books. So do not seek for proof from outside for you will need [to make] the journey to the seventh heaven. Seek after the truth closer to yourself, inside yourself' (ibid.).

In the context of the Arab language, the Sufi experience is not merely important because of its search (for knowledge/truth) but also because of the writing it engendered. The Sufi vision has been expressed in poetry, in metric verse and prose and in poetic language, as well as the language of research and explanation. In terms of its literature, it is an innovative movement, which has pushed back the boundaries of poetry, adding to its rhythmic forms other forms of versification that modern critics call *qasidat-al-nathr*, or prose poems. Arab literary criticism has to change its concepts of poetry and establish new ways of defining and understanding it, but this has not happened. Sufi literature has had to wait more than ten centuries to find people – and even now they remain rare – who will make the effort to read and understand it in a fresh light.

Sufism is distinctive in that, in its search for the absolute, it resorts to poetry when it wishes to express its most profound feelings; this has traditionally been the ultimate means of expressing a sense of nearness to and knowledge of the absolute. Do not those who follow the orthodox religious *shari'a* use it as proof in their refutation of Sufism, for they reject poetry and place a clear and antithetical limit between it and religion, especially on intellectual grounds? Sufism sees poetical writing as a primary way of explaining its mysteries, and poetic language as a primary means to knowledge. This is a continuation of what went before Islam and revelation, and represents the retrieval of the trusted link between poetry and the absence. The Sufis use art in their doctrines about God and existence and man: figurative language and style, symbolism, metaphor, imagery, rhythm, wordplay; the reader experiences their experience, and has a glimpse of their horizons through their art. Those readers who enter this world reliant on the ostensible external meaning of phrases will find it difficult. To put it another way, it is virtually impossible to enter the Sufi world by way of explanation, for allusion rather than explanation is the main portal.

The language of the Sufis is, to some extent, poetic, and the poetical nature of this language is represented by the fact that everything in it is symbolic: everything in it is itself and something else. The beloved, for example, may mean the beloved, but it may also mean rose, or wine or water or God. It is an image of the universe and its revelations. The same thing can be said about the sky or earth or God. Things in the Sufi vision are dissimilar quiddities, different harmonies. Thus Sufi language differs from that of the *shari'a* in that, in the *shari'a,* things represent themselves and nothing else.

In this language, Sufism creates a world inside the world, in which its creations are contained, which is born and grows, which comes and goes, which flares up and dies down. In this world the timeless is embraced in a living present.

Whereas in *shari'a* language things are said as they are in a complete and finite way, the poetical language of the Sufis gives only an image of them, because it is referring to the absolute, which cannot be said or described or understood completely. It is impossible to express infinity except by using finite action; speech is finite and those who speak are finite, so the ability of speech to describe infinity can only be indicative and symbolic. For that reason Sufi doctrine, like poetic expression, remains metaphysical and does not ever represent the truth in the same way as does religious *shari'a* expression.

The language of Sufism also differs from the religious *shari'a* language in another way. The latter is essentially a language of explanation, while the former is one of love. The former loves things without necessarily understanding them, while the relationship of *shari'a* language to things and the universe is one of understanding, knowing and valuation rather than love. Love itself is not expressed but experienced. You can convey images of it but, in essence, it is like the absolute, impossible to talk about, because it is beyond the borders of logic and reason. In other words, it is beyond speech. The poem is merely an attempt on the part of man to put into speech symbolically or figuratively what he is unable to say. Reason and logic do not regulate poetry. If it is a true poem, it cannot be classified as rational or logical. Poetry, like something spoken, cannot be understood or explained definitively. Understanding can help to illuminate it but does not exhaustively explain its content. What cannot be described cannot be fully known. The unknown and the indescribable converge. Thus every reader finds his own poem in every poem he reads and it is the same thing in Sufi writing.

But why does man try to say things that he knows are impossible to say? Perhaps the answer lies in the fact that man longs for things beyond his ken or understanding. Perhaps he tries to create a oneness between himself and the absolute and to feel that he is part of an unending universe and that, like the universe, he has no end. Perhaps he wishes to say that instead of two, there is only one. In this respect, in particular, the language of Sufism differs from that of the *shari'a*; the former originates from the Sufis' attempts to become one with God, while the latter has its roots in the orthodox experience of describing and proscribing, which confirms its complete separation and detachment from the absolute.

# 5

It would be difficult to write an article in the Sufi manner. Such an article would be superficial, descriptive and bland. However, it is possible to write an article in the Surrealist manner and such articles exist. Breton himself wrote such articles, as did others, despite the fact that Surrealism did not present itself as a dogma as Aragon announced. Although it contained ideas, which could be considered as founding principles, it never permitted any prior form of control on its subsequent progress. 'We must look to the future,' says Aragon, concluding his words in this context (Maurice Nadeau, *The History of Surrealism*, Cambridge, Mass., Belknap Press, 1989, p. 57).

I believe that the significance of Sufism today does not lie in its written dogma (philosophical literature), so much as the path it follows to attain this writing. It lies in the gnostic domain that it has established and in the principles that it has produced, and they are principles that are peculiar to it and different from those used in research and discovery. It lies in the vast spaces that it has opened up and in the ways it speaks about them, in language in particular. The same thing can be said about the Surrealists. In terms of Arab culture, the importance of the Sufi contribution lies in its re-reading of the religious texts and the attribution to them of other meanings and dimensions; this in turn permits a new reading of the literary, philosophical and political legacy, which has led to a fresh look at language, not only in the religious context but also as a tool of revelation and expression. Sufis have gone beyond the legacy of the 'established principles' to set up the legacy of the mysteries. Another form of knowledge has been established and another intellectual domain.

Because of this revolt against sectarianism, Sufism has been accused of heresy and atheism. Its identification as heresy permits a religious reading of the social struggle, which has marginalized the Sufi movement and separated it from the socio-philosophical body. Sufism has become the other pariah within society. Their description of themselves as the 'people of the concealed' as opposed to the 'people of the apparent' can be traced to that. It is a form of defence and a form of justification, especially as the apparent denies the concealed, not only on religious grounds but also on political and social grounds. This view of heresy provides us with an idea of how the ideological and social were conjoined, and enables us to see how the socio-cultural body was created.

This vision and reading also provide us with an opportunity to understand the movement of change or progress in society, in respect to its deeply rooted and unchanging beliefs and the role played by thought – heretical thought, in particular – in this movement. Although heretics and atheists, members of religious cults associated with them and those who are marginalized socially and ideologically, such as cultural and racial minorities and the insane, etc, do not represent the social body and do not claim such representation for themselves, they are nevertheless storing up a power that is a much more able means of moving and changing the social body.

6

The Surrealists, like the Sufis, bring together writing and life. To give an example, it is not sufficient to write poetry, but life should be lived as well. This stance opposes the prevailing view of the time, which had separated writing and life. Before the Surrealists, Baudelaire and Mallarmé championed poetry at the expense of bourgeois culture and capitalism. Wealth provided the yardstick for this culture, on which it based its values. Baudelaire and Mallarmé made poetry the only thing of value. Baudelaire put it in place of religion, and Mallarmé saw it as the supreme value (Véronique Bartoli-Anglard, *Le Surréalisme*, Paris, Nathan, 1989, p. 10).

André Breton tries hard to reconcile the two demands: 'the

search for an absolute being and the desire to act in the concrete. The other members of the group do not submit themselves to the same dialectic; the traditional opposition between theory and practice in this case transforms itself into a conflict between poetic language and action, between the marvellous and Marxism.' The Surrealists see that art 'has given man a means through which he will be able to surpass himself in the arena of what is human. It must offer him the riches of a new wonder.' The Surrealists therefore 'venerate those thinkers who have exploited the resources of the imagination and distanced themselves from society; they admire the Romantics and those authors on the margins of society, who have extolled the virtues of rebellion or who have engaged in fantasy and esotericism' (ibid., p. 11).

The Romantics before them had postulated the pre-eminence of the interior world over sordid reality. The poetry, which has a philosophical dimension such as that of Victor Hugo and Alfred de Vigny, is very often epic, and suggests an idea that is speculative, fabulous and concrete at the same time. The Romantics 'elevate sensibility, imagination, dream and passion over reason and logic' (ibid.).

The most profound way in which the Romantics influence the Surrealists is in their view of the poet. They say, 'The poet is a prophet who reads the text of the world and deciphers the laws of the universe in an intuitive manner' (ibid., p. 12). The Surrealists count Hugo, Nerval, Hölderlin, Novalis, Coleridge and Blake as among their most important precursors in this field.

Symbolism plays an important part in the development of Surrealism. With Baudelaire, poetry takes on a mystical role through which he tries to establish an understanding of the correspondence between the visible and the invisible. Rimbaud goes further and makes the poet a visionary, who practises an alchemy of words. He thinks that poetry on its own is a means of transforming mankind; how can the poet live his poetry if not by re-inventing life?

'Transforming life': the Surrealists take on this aphorism and hold on to it; like Rimbaud, they want to attain the impossible. And this desire to attain the absolute is one of the obligatory requests and fundamental goals of the Surrealists.

The Surrealists recognize themselves in those marginalized writers who 'have affirmed their special cultural position *vis-à-vis* the restrictions of the official order, and who include, among others, the Libertines who wrote in the seventeenth century and the Illuminists such as Sade from the eighteenth century as well as thinkers and writers who were and remain unrecognized in French literature. Among the little-known writers they have rescued from oblivion are Aloysius Bertrand and Petrus Borel (ibid., p. 13). The Surrealists recognize themselves in Sade because they believe that absolute love finds fulfilment in the perfect union between soul and body. Their refusal of the Christian notion of separation of flesh and spirit is linked to their denunciation of the notion of inherent guilt attached to physical desire.

The Surrealists have helped make known the work of Lautréamont through his *Chants de Maldoror*, which expressed a new concept in writing. They hold him up as a great modern poet because he ridiculed all conventions. He not only criticized bourgeois society, but also challenged romanticism through parody and questioned all forms of thought (ibid., pp. 13–14).

The Surrealists seek to recapture the magic of the world by implementing the psychic forces of the individual and getting back in touch with the magical use of language and attaining the philosopher's stone, at the same time as acting concretely, practising self-criticism and criticism of society (ibid., p. 15).

Surrealism is much influenced by esotericism, a perennial philosophy of what is contained in the order of knowledge: a gnosis (intuitive knowledge, suprarational, transcendental) through which man can re-establish a universal metaphysic. At the same time this influence goes back to criticizing the view of the rational world and reflection on language (ibid., p. 15).

At the dawn of the twentieth century, an anti-positive turn-around appears in a world already rocked by Nietzsche, with Bergson's writings on the vital impulse, intuition and memory, Freud's new concept of the psyche and the subconscious, and research by the Futurists into language and a rethinking of the whole concept of art (ibid., p. 16). It becomes a question of re-examining the accepted norms, the ways in which things are seen and the ways of speaking about them. A new spirit is born and defines itself in opposition to the traditional idea of art as a complete form, which follows fixed principles (ibid.).

However, the Surrealists do not re-examine language but, on the contrary, keep faith with it. They wish to change the way of using it, so as to be able the better to celebrate life (ibid., p. 17).

The Surrealists announce their break with ancient society and its foundations and morals, its aesthetics and its positivism. Their goal is to bring about a complete man in a union of the conscious and unconscious. They use systematic and scientific methods to exploit the unconscious through experiences as diverse as dreams, madness, marvels and hallucinatory states of mind. Poetry becomes the instrument of this research into the interior. They use the discoveries of Freud. The unconscious is part of psychic life, as is the conscious. It is necessary to free man from his guilt and not to censure his desires.

It is up to man to change his relationship with reality, and this change will come about through language, through a new rapport between language and the object described. The meaning will have to be sought for beneath the overtly visible (ibid., p. 18).

The knowledge of the world demands a re-examination of reason limited to itself. Why should everything in man be rational? Why not accept that there exist infinite possibilities, not yet discovered, which could give a purely human solution to the question of man? (ibid., p. 19).

To begin with, it is necessary to renounce the principles of causality and affirm the supreme power of the unconscious over logic and determinism. It is not a question of creating a new form of art but rather of exploring the unknown resources of the human being. We should not limit the eruption of anarchic forces but exercise our critical faculties to change the concrete condition of life. By overcoming schematic opposition, we will realize the whole man, as Hegel, whom Breton admires so much, has said. Restoring the reign of creative imagination will enable the individual to express himself in an authentic way. Language is both an instrument of communication with others and also a means of liberating oneself internally and externally.

The Surrealists are very interested in the Orient. They see in it a reservoir of spiritual forces and energy, which serves as a permanent revolt. Breton and Aragon regard metaphysical reflection as particularly important. So for the Surrealists, the Orient is both a mysterious domain and the place where desire has freed itself through the Russian revolution. René Guénon, who had a determining influence on them, believes that the West is going through a stage he calls the Dark Ages. He believes the Orient has escaped this stage because it has retained its esoteric tradition and principles (ibid., p. 20).

Reflecting on the Orient allows them to re-examine the ideas of the predecessors of Socrates, in particular Heraclitus, who does not recognize the concept of contradiction. They believe that, 'Everything is in everything.' The Surrealists subscribe to this irrational way of thinking, which is close to the view held by Pythagorists and members of secret religions, and seek to release the secrets that lie behind logical speech, by detecting its capacity in its early stages and, through the living word, that of the myth that gives a concrete form to perceptions.

7

These encounters and intersections, sometimes opaque, other times apparent, between Sufism and Surrealism are what I will try to uncover in this book. The point at issue is not who has influenced whom, or the extension or interaction between them, so much as the issue of that inner tension shared by all creators who find themselves travelling along similar paths in search of a solution, but who, because they are attracted by different things, attain different goals.

Sufism and Surrealism allow us to see another side of things, the absence and the presence: the absence of man and the presence of mechanics, the absence of the heart and the presence of reason, the absence of nature and the presence of industry.

## 8

'With this transcendental thought, which has been cheated by a beginning and end whose name is God, it appears that there is something that will continue in modern culture: the motion of travelling without end as if the experience, which is no longer able to be based upon a belief in God, has preserved the form of traditional Sufism, though not its content … and when the traveller has basically no anchorage, he will have no point of departure and no point of arrival. He will submit to a nameless desire like a drunken boat.'[11] Thus Michel de Certau ends his book about the poetess Catherine Bozi. In my opinion, these are words that can be applied as much to the Surrealist experience as to the Sufi. The former has preserved the 'form' of the latter, in order to achieve a changing output. Their paths are one, but the revelation is different.

## 9

Will we find in both Sufism and Surrealism a formula or a new way of thinking in which both sides will embrace the other?

PART ONE

Sufism and Surrealism

# Knowledge

Unchanging knowledge is unchanging ignorance.
*al-Niffari*
Reject reason, stay always with reality.
*al-Shabastri (13th century)*
Light is a veil.
*Ibn 'Arabi*

1

Knowledge in the most profound and basic sense of the word is what connects the I to existence, the self to the object; the greater the knowledge, the smaller the distance between the two. Knowledge therefore is the connection that unites the knowing self to what is known.

According to the Sufis, existence is not an external subject that can be understood using external tools such as reason or logic. In fact, the use of logical and analytical reasoning to get a better understanding of existence only increases man's sense of loss and confusion. It distances him from himself as well as from existence. According to the Sufis, employing such a cognitive tool is like looking at the sun with the naked eye; the eye is blinded by the sun's brightness and the seer is more ignorant as a result. In the same way, if we depend on reason for a knowledge of existence, it will only make us more ignorant. True knowledge or gnosis comes from knowing something from within. It negates the distance between the knower and the thing known and allows the knower to realize its true essence. We can know existence, according to Sufi doctrine, only by witnessing it and practising it, i.e. through presence, taste or illumination, which are Sufi terms.

Knowledge in the Sufi sense of the word begins with the Absolute. Shibli says, 'Knowledge begins with God (the Absolute) and it is everlasting and infinite.' At this level, the knower does not have a state, like other creatures. At this level, as al-Bastami says, the knower's 'depiction' is obliterated and 'his identity is annihilated by an identity other than his, and his traces concealed by traces other than his.' This knowledge will not produce absolute certainty and tranquillity as is believed. The aim of knowledge, according to Sahil ibn Abdullah, 'is to make you surprised and confused', because, as Dhu al-Nun al-Masri says, 'those who have the greatest knowledge of God (the Absolute) are the most confused about him.' Thus he himself becomes the absolute, unrestrained by any state. Were we to ask, 'Who is the knower?', the answer would be, 'He was here and he has gone.'

However, this knowledge cannot be achieved while the knower is conscious of his ego and his I-ness as something external, a living manifestation embodied in the now. In fact, the ego is an obstacle to the acquisition of knowledge because its individuality is a wall that divides the knower from the known. It is possible to know existence truly only by overcoming the ego and reaching a state in which the conscious self completely vanishes. The Sufis describe this state as *fana'* (annihilation). *Fana'*, in this sense, means the finest and richest state of permanence in existence. For *fana'* is the removal of any impediments and the obliteration of the veil. In *fana'*, existence loses its concerns, its limitations and its chains and returns to its origins, limitless and unqualified. In *fana'*, therefore, a complete congruence is achieved between the subjective state of the knower and the objective state of the known world. External things, that is, the specifications of existence, are links and ties, based on illusion. Through *fana'* the veil of illusion is rent apart, and from this tearing apart comes permanence in existence. *Fana'* is the 'fall of bad properties' and *baqa'* (permanence in existence) is 'the raising of properties that are praiseworthy'. Al-Jami ordains that, in order to be aware, 'You should distance yourself from yourself.' Another Sufi says, 'Inasmuch as you are alien to yourself, you will be able to acquire knowledge.'

In order to attain the state of *fana'*, the Sufi travels and meditates, restoring the many to the one, that is, working to purify his soul of any other connections. *Fana'* is a personal, internal experience, which at the same time is an experience of being, inasmuch as it reveals being to itself. It reveals through the experience of discovery and disclosure. And if revelation in the strict Sufi meaning of the word 'is the manifestation of the essence in the veils of the names and qualities that are sent down from heaven', then it means knowledge or gnosis, knowledge of the Absolute. This knowledge is the *mahu* (obliteration) of the knower in what is known. Shibli says, 'If I am with Him, I am myself, but I am obliterated in what He is.' Nevertheless, this obliteration is life. Al-Junaid refers to it as follows: 'The Absolute will make you die through him and will make you live.' In this state, the Sufi attains utter clarity. 'Nothing troubles him and everything is clear to him.' Thus, by negating everything apart from God, he is led to the Absolute, to God.

There are several stages or degrees of *fana'*, or knowledge of the Absolute: *mukashafat* (uncovering), *tajalli* (revelation) and *mushahadat* (perception and sight of God).

*Mukashafat* (uncovering) means that the Absolute is hidden, veiled by things, and that He will remain unknown until these veils vanish. Created objects are like a veil that comes between man and his creator. Man will not attain the Absolute nor penetrate his mysteries unless he goes through a physical and mental struggle, which will lead to the obliteration of everything that separates him materially from Him.

Through *mukashafat* (uncovering), he achieves knowledge of the beauty and majesty of God (the Absolute), a knowledge of the mysteries of divine wisdom, divine words and divine presence and oneness with the Absolute.

In *tajalli* (divine revelation), the veil dissolves when the divine light appears or God reveals himself through his light and with it reveals divine things. God is light and its rays are his creation. Every being, as something originating with God, is an illumined being. The spirit, for example, is light but it is dim because it is joined to the body.

*Tajalli* (revelation) comes about either through contemplation or directly through God's grace. In the case of contemplation, divine light pierces the body and enters the soul. The body is unable to bear it and the person is affected by dizziness. However, when revelation comes about through God's grace, the person is filled with peace and calm. Through divine revelation, the darkness that envelops the secret path of ecstasy disappears.

*Mushahadat* (the witnessing of God) ordains that the veils that conceal the divine presence should dissolve and that the spirit be illuminated with revelation and that nothing should remain apart from the vision. *Mushahadat* is direct knowledge of the Absolute, obtained through seeing him and experiencing him with the eye. Since *mukashafat* (the uncovering) is 'removing the cover' that veils the divine light and since *tajalli* (revelation) is the encounter with the lights of mysteries, *mushahadat* (witnessing of God) is the reflection or the presence of these lights in the heart, which radiate off it as if off a pure mirror. These lights initially appear like a fleeting flash of lightning on the surface of the heart, and then bit by bit increase in power until they are so bright that they have no equal in any form in the light of the material world.

*Inkhitaf* (ecstasy) accompanies or follows this stage, and is the most distinct and the most exalted in character of any of the states of the inner life. It is the primary mystical grace. It does not come at will or through preparation but unexpectedly and suddenly, a mystical grace from God, which is destined for those individuals who are perfect. It also comes to others who work and prepare for it.

Ibn 'Arabi distinguishes six stages of ecstasy:

> In the first stage, the Sufi loses awareness of human actions (for they are the work of God).
>
> In the second stage, he loses awareness of his powers and attributes, which are appropriated by God. God, not the Sufi, sees, listens, thinks and wants with these senses (not 'we are thinking', but 'we are thought', as Rimbaud said).
>
> In the third stage, awareness of the self disappears, and all a Sufi's thoughts are taken up with the contemplation of God and divine things. The Sufi forgets that it is he who is thinking.
>
> In the fourth stage, the Sufi no longer feels that God is the one who is thinking about him or through him.
>
> In the fifth stage, his contemplation of God makes him forget everything apart from him.
>
> In the sixth stage, the field of consciousness narrows, the qualities of God become non-existent and God alone as an absolute being with no ties or qualities or names is revealed to the Sufi in ecstasy.

Before losing consciousness, the Sufi feels spiritually elated. He is filled with a sense of physical languor as if he is no longer in possession of his body. It is a refreshing tiredness in which his limbs do not wish to move.

Ecstasy is accompanied by other states: attainment of God is a state that some Sufis are not strong enough to bear. It is a state that controls and takes hold of the person in such a manner that they lose their independence and freedom. Some of them return to their normal state of being after having achieved ecstasy, while others remain lost or mad for the rest of their lives.

Principally, Sufis seek to achieve ecstasy, not because of the ecstasy itself or the states that precede, accompany or follow it, but because it is a means of adding to their knowledge and becoming more perfect.

2

In the Sufi vision, therefore, the Absolute (God, Being) manifests himself in two ways: the apparent and the concealed (the inner and the outer, the conscious and unconscious). The apparent is clear, rational. The concealed is hidden, heartfelt. The Absolute in its concealed form is unknown and not known, a continuous mystery. In its apparent form, it is known and embraces all things.

The Sufis describe the Absolute as 'the hidden treasure', recalling what Lao Tsu called 'the door to marvels which cannot be enumerated.'

When it comes to understanding the inner world, we should distinguish between two views of existence. I will rely here on the distinction that Toshiko Izutsu uses in his book *The Concept of Perpetual Creation in Islamic Mysticism and Zen Buddhism*, Tehran, 1977). I will summarize what he says: The ordinary common view of things (this is the rational view) regards quiddities and essences as existing, or it sees things that exist but does not see pure existence. Existence is contained in these existing things and what lies beyond them through their quiddities. It is a quality or attribute of these quiddities. This view of existence is associated with the essentialist philosophical school.

As for the extraordinary view, it regards existing things as existence and things and essences as attributes pertaining to it. The flower, for example, exists only as an attribute of existence. In this view, things exist figuratively, through their ties, relationships and attributes. This view of reality is associated with existentialism (Izutsu, pp. 58–59).

The writer goes on to explain that there is no temporal disjunction between the inner and the external, between the Absolute and its revelations. There is no disjunction between the appearance of the sun and the appearance of its light or between the sun and its light, although the light comes after the sun and the sun exists first. In the same way, there is no distinction between the sea and the wave. The wave is a different form of the sea; it cannot exist independently of the sea. Nor can the sea exist without the wave. The sea appears in each wave in a different form. But the true nature of the sea remains one, both in the waves and in their undulations. 'There is no distinction between the sea and the wave (the inner and the external, the Absolute and reality, reality and essence)', as Haydar Amali asserts.

3

The Surrealists have practical knowledge of experiences similar to those moments of ecstasy described by the Sufis, and frequently write about them. Spontaneous visions occur during moments such as these. Aragon describes the state of the mind that results from it as follows: 'First of all, each of us regarded himself as the object of a particular disturbance and struggled against this disturbance. Soon its nature was revealed. Everything occurred as if the mind, having reached this crest of the unconscious, had lost the power to recognize its position. In it subsisted images that assumed form and became the substance of reality. They experienced themselves according to this relation as a perceptible force. They thus assumed the characteristics of visual, audible and tactile hallucinations. We experienced the full power of these images. We lost the power to manipulate them and became the domain and their subjects. We held out our hands to phantoms, in bed, just before falling asleep or

in the street with eyes wide open, with all the machinery of terror'
(Maurice Nadeau, *The History of Surrealism*, p. 46).

This recalls what the Sufis call 'miracles' (*al-karamat*); it is well
known that it is sufficient for a person to cross the threshold between
the conscious and the unconscious, which exists in everyone, to see
another reality; this is richer and broader than conscious reality and
contains intuitive knowledge, desires and unlimited and endless
pleasure, beneath which conscious feelings that are constrained and
enclosed by daily life collapse.

In the *First Surrealist Manifesto* (1924), which is considered the
most fundamental of the Surrealist documents, Breton lays out
his psychological and philosophical understanding and principles.
We can see from it that he attributes particular importance to
imagination and fantasy by describing them as the seat of freedom
and its primary component, in particular free thought.

At the same time as promoting imagination and fantasy, he
demotes the value of reason and logic, which can be applied to
problems of secondary interest only. Absolute rationalism, which
remains in fashion, as he puts it, allows man to consider only those
facts and issues that form a mere part of his experience. Breton goes
on to say that in today's world, under the pretext of civilization
and progress, man is deaf to any search for the truth that is not
based on reason or logic, on the grounds that it is superstition or
myth (*First Surrealist Manifesto*, p. 316).[1] Breton establishes a link
between dreams and original thought, which is present in man's
inner self. In the dream state, laws of logic and reason dissolve.
The dream immerses man in a special universe, a world made up
of internal images and an unconscious tide. When man ceases to
sleep, he is completely at the mercy of his memory (ibid., p. 317),
and the memory cancels the value of the dream and kills it. Breton
then asks whether the dream state is not the closest approximation
to original thought and the profound nature of man. Why should
we not concede to the dream, Breton asks, what we sometimes
refuse to attribute to reality – the weight of absolute certainty?
Why should we not expect more of the dream than we do from

consciousness? Cannot dreams as well be applied to the solution of life's fundamental problems? When confronted with the value or importance of the dream state, wakefulness appears to be nothing more than a complete obstacle (ibid., p. 318). Wakefulness in this context is a state of absence from the truth, or a state in which truths are partial and marginalized, distant from the vital and positive centre of thought. Therefore it is necessary, in asserting the unity of man with this new understanding, to embrace the tangible facts and include them in the realm of the unconscious, which can be made clear through dreams and automatic or involuntary writing.[2] Breton stresses that the dream and reality, outwardly so contradictory, will be resolved into a kind of absolute reality, a sur-reality. This can be compared to what the Sufis refer to as the character of uniqueness (*unicité* in French) or oneness between the inner and the apparent.

If the dream presents a new form of reality to man, allowing him new ways of linking himself to existence and opening up fresh horizons, then of necessity everything that he realizes by these similarities takes on a primary importance. Thus the Surrealists reveal the significance of magic, astrology and the esoteric – the mystical legacy, which includes Buddhism. In the *Second Surrealist Manifesto*, Breton acclaims Gnosticism and ritual secrets and calls for a return to the profound and true mystery, peculiar to Surrealism (p. 821). He says it is up to the Surrealists to recognize the esoteric sciences, such as astrology and natural magic (ibid.), and he stresses the need to 'search out what is secret', pointing to the fact that Surrealism has been entrusted with this secret as if it is a prophetic message. In the second manifesto, he describes how he and Eluard and Aragon were born under harmonious astrological signs (Uranus and Saturn). Surrealism therefore appears to have been inspired 'legitimately, naturally or cosmically'. In order to emphasize the 'secret' and the importance of searching for it, he once asked, 'How can it happen that the externalities meet and become one when each of them is separate from the other and has an independent cause? Why is the light that comes from this union alive and vehemently vital, if it is so fleeting?' (*Entretiens*, p. 141).

Thus the fundamental goal of Surrealism, which is also that of the Sufis, is the union of contradictions, or the 'unity of existence', by which I mean the oneness between the essence and the object, between the external world and inner knowledge. If all the components of the dream are drawn from reality then it is not incompatible with action.

Breton sees the poet of the future as someone who is able to bypass the idea of separation between action and dream. Man will attain a state of bliss, and this state will be produced through unity in one being of everything that is apparent from the outside and the inside; this is represented in the action of loving, where there is no distinction between the sweetness of feeling and the passions of the soul.

It is a union of opposites: water and fire. The Surrealists adopted the words of Heraclitus who said, 'The sea is the first transmutation of fire.'

The phrase 'the union of opposites' leads on to the phrase 'the oneness of being', though among the Surrealists this oneness is controversial and much written about. As Michel Carrouges points out, Surrealism ended up by embracing different realities of elements as a whole in a supreme concept that overcomes the contradictions.

This supreme concept is what Breton refers to as the 'supreme point', defining it as follows: 'Everything leads to the belief that there exists a certain point of the mind at which life and death, the real and the imaginary, the past and the future, the communicable and the incommunicable, the high and the low, are not perceived as contradictions. It would be vain to attribute to Surrealism any other motive than the hope of determining this point' (*Second Manifesto*, p. 781).

Marcel Raymond defines this supreme point as follows: 'Surrealism in the widest sense of the word represents the most recent attempt to break with existing things and to put others in their place that are fully effective and functioning and whose moving contours are implicitly inscribed in the depths of their being ... Never before in France has a school of poets brought together in such a way and so very consciously the critical issues of poetry and existence.'

This supreme point is the place in which the inner being, the essence and the outer being, the subject, meet. At this point, we go beyond the allegorical, which denies inferiority in the name of superiority, and we relinquish materialism, which denies the superior in the name of the inferior. The inferior and the superior are equal at this point. They emerge with one meaning. It is the point at which things of all kinds are in harmony, despite their variety, and between reality and what lies behind it. The divine powers, which Nietzsche dreams of reclaiming and which the Arab Sufis experience, are gathered together in it. It is a restatement of the theory of *al-hulul* (God and man becoming one) and the theory of the oneness of existence.

We describe 'the supreme point' as a higher reality; essential reality and objective reality are only revelations of it.

It is difficult to define this point. The question, 'What is it?' is the Surrealist question par excellence. It is also the Sufi question. It is a question that is characterized by the fact that it does not have an answer. It is infinite. There is no limit to infinity. This supreme point is not a question that can be answered. It is only a horizon for the traveller to head towards.

At this supreme point, the impediments from the world of externalities (the rational, the objective, etc) disappear, and we achieve gnosis. Dualism ends, contradictions vanish. Dualism is what keeps man in ignorance, walling him in with individual, social and classical expressions, keeping him a stranger. At this supreme point, we go beyond alienation and attain our true selves.

When we attain our true selves, we attain 'knowledge', the gnosis born out of the fundamental relationship between being and gnosis. This gnosis is an awakening, which generates a memory of what we were before we became lost in the world of tangible things.

It can be seen therefore that the Surrealists talk about the existence of a domain that lies beyond the bounds of reason and which man does not exploit. Human beings are not aware that the events of daily life are the result of a chain of causes the secrets of which elude them. It is sufficient for them to cast a fresh eye on reality to perceive that these decisive causes are not subject to any form of logic. The Surrealist object appears as the point of convergence between apparent chance and hidden causality. Why is man not aware of this hidden causality? Because he perceives objects as purely utilitarian. Everything, however, has a use other than that generally attributed to it. The instrumental function of the object has to give way to its poetic function. Rational man only possesses a superficial view of the world. If he is to attain the marvellous and extraordinary, then he will have to change his way of thinking about the world that surrounds him (Bartoli-Anglard: *Le Surréalisme*, p. 82).

Breton rehabilitates absurdity, neurosis, insanity and contemplation as means that have been given to us and through which we can realize the origins of psychic life. Such tools enable us to see things and the unknown links between them and allow us to realize the relationship between the inner truths and the external reality (ibid., p. 83). At the beginning of *Nadja*, Breton asks, 'Who am I?', and replies, 'I am the one whom I haunt.' He could also have replied, 'I am the one who haunts me.' Nadja is beautiful; she is the daughter of the mysterious Orient, the *djinn* of objective chance. Nadja is Surrealist (ibid., p. 85).

Objective chance, insanity and fortune-tellers all bear witness to the gap that exists between man and real life and the continuing distance between them. Breton believes that to recapture such lost spontaneity, we must return to lyrical and pre-logical words such as myths (ibid., p. 87).

This all lends emphasis to the fact that Surrealism can trace its roots to an ideological inheritance that cannot be described in any way as rational or as Western in the current sense of the word, in spite of the fact that it was inspired by Freud in particular and Marx in a more general way. The reasons for this lie in the gnostic methods upon which they rely, which are completely different from those that make up the cultural identity of the West.

Most of the people whom Breton lists as influences on Surrealism do not come from either the logical or the rational tradition. They include Heraclitus, Abelard, Meister Eckhart, Rousseau, Swift, Sade and Lautréamont, to name but a few. In addition, he also lays claim to the influence of such non-rational cultures as the Celts and the Hopi Indians, as well as magical arts, secret rites, Gnostics, the anarchists, the spiritualists, mental illness and cults. The cognitive procedure of the Surrealists lays emphasis, for all that, on the bringing together of realities that have no logical or rational link, to produce groups that permit new knowledge and new truths.

He sees the importance of the Celtic culture, for example, as lying, on the one hand, in its connection to 'symbolic forests' and, on the other, in its complete break with the Latin tradition (*Surrealism and Photography*, Paris, Gallimard, 1981, p. 337).

He also notes that Baudelaire is linked to the Gnostic mysteries, through his preoccupation with the correspondence between the visible and the invisible in the universe. Baudelaire tries to use poetry to uncover the hidden relationship between the apparent and the concealed worlds, in order to overcome the pain of existence (according to some of his critics).

Just as Baudelaire attempts to uncover other hidden worlds and reveal the ways in which they correspond to our world, Mallarmé attempts to summon up the invisible, that which lies beyond the world, in order to convey his search for the transparency of the I in the movement of the universe: 'I must tell you that I am not my self now, and I am no longer the person (Stéphane) whom you used to know, but I have become one of the paths through which the spiritual universe has chosen to show itself and to present what was my self, pierced from side to side.'[3] These words of Mallarmé, which might have been said by any Arab Sufi, influenced Breton.

4

The Christian mystics, as well as many other writers in the West, know such moments of revelation and write about them. They are all agreed that a primary condition for the appearance of the flash of illumination is that man withdraw into the self, where the inner person dwells, and that he live in it, and cut his ties with the outside world and with rational and descriptive path of knowledge. This withdrawal enables him to strengthen this presence of and in himself so he can better penetrate the depths of existence.

Georges Bataille describes this withdrawal in *Acéphale* (1939, p. 14):

> I abandon myself to peace, until I am annihilated.
> The noises of the struggle lose themselves in death as rivers
>     are lost in the sea and splinters of stars are lost in the sky.
> The power of combat is accomplished in the silence of
>     action.
> I enter into peace as into an unknown desire.
> I plunge into this unknown desire.
> I become myself in this unknown desire.

He talks about his transformation at the moment of intoxication or ecstasy:

> I am transformed into endless flight, outside myself, as if my life is running like a slow river through the ink of the sky. At that moment, I am no longer myself, but what comes out of me attains a presence, which has no limitations to imprison it in their embrace, and which appears itself to resemble the loss of myself. (*Le Coupable*, 1944, 2nd imprint, p. 18)

Bataille goes on to say:

In ecstasy [delirium], I see the exterior but every sign of order – the leaves of the tree, for example, which are in front of me oppress me.

But he is easily able to see the sky and the clouds because 'such things are fragmented'. For in delirium, everything vanishes, even God. He says, 'I imagine the emptiness looks like a flame.' The absence of the thing reveals the flame, which intoxicates and illuminates (*On Nietzsche*, 1945, p. 282).

Bataille therefore disregards and disdains reason and logic. In this, his position forms part of the fundamental ideative stance adopted by the Surrealist movement in their uncovering of what we shall call the inner continent and the tools that allowed them to discover it.

André Masson says, 'Reason is the most powerful enemy of the spirit ... As far as we young Surrealists were concerned in 1924, reason was the great "prostitute". We believed that followers of Descartes and Voltaire and other members of the intelligentsia had done nothing but hang on to established and obsolete values ... I would add objectively that the game – the serious game – added to this immersion in the night (in what German Romantics call the nocturnal side of things) and the desirable summons of the marvellous' (see also Masson, *Ecrits*, Paris, Hermann, 1976, pp. 16–17).

Crével says that reason, 'paralysed and paralysing, places its opacity between the thinker, sitting down in order to think, and the matter in motion, the matter in the process of change, as if this matter is never matter for thought. Reason, this pawn, soils everything with its cautious reality' (ibid., p. 161).

According to Sufism and Surrealism, the error of reason and logic lies in the fact that they concentrate on trivial things and claim that they have the answer to everything. Reason and logic treat existence as a problem that must have a solution, as the answer is deduced rationally and logically. Sufism and Surrealism, on the other hand, look on existence as something mysterious, and they are preoccupied with the question of how to become one with this mystery. The absence of answers here demonstrates a preoccupation with becoming one with existence. The presence of answers here demonstrates a preoccupation with exerting control over existence, i.e. it is separate; the first state denotes love and the second state supremacy.

Man is betrayed through his search for answers; they restrict him, i.e. they cut off his freedom. Answers separate man from himself, from his essence: man is a language – searching for the other, for the thing, not in order to make it submit to his knowledge of it, but rather to join with it, in equality and love. Answers suppose there is nothing in existence, which is unknown and leads to claims of falsehood and complete error. In existence there are things that we do not know, which we cannot know rationally or logically, but can only become joined and one with.

As for daily collective reason, it not only suppresses and restrains man but it also betrays him.

Reason limits, and therefore its answers limit. When we define something, we negate it – in the sense that we enclose it in brackets – the definition – and negate what lies outside it. The definition is a negation, as Spinoza says. When you define God, you negate him, because you make him equal to things that have been defined. Defining man or existence denies the essence of both of them. Man, like existence, is a free, potential and diverse reality, not a reality that is finite and fettered.

Man lights up everything, so how can he illumine if he is limited? From this point of view, freedom is the essence of man, and there is something infinite in man: it does not become less, nor can it be known completely and finally.

5

In his well-known article on mysticism,[5] William James sets down four properties, which apply as much to Surrealism as to Sufism.

1. Ineffability: The spiritual states of the mystic cannot be described in words and therefore cannot be communicated but must be experienced. This is particularly true when they are linked to the unconscious. How wrong we are to judge such states from their external appearance or to assess them rationally when there is nothing rational about them!

2. Noetic quality: Although mystic states are conscious-passive, they are gnostic states, which penetrate the depths of truth that the mind has not probed before.

3. Transience: Such states do not last for a long time, and in most case memory fails to describe them, once they are over.

4. Passivity: As soon as such states occur, the person in the state loses his will and feels that he is possessed or taken over by a higher power over which he has no control; this characteristic is associated with particular manifestations such as prophecy, ecstasy, automatic writing and trance.

Henri Michaux repeats William James's words in his own particular fashion. Through using drugs, this poet attained the same state as that attained by the Sufis through physical exertion and without the use of drugs. In describing this state, which he calls obliteration or effacement and in which rational control is absent and where thought works in its mysterious spaces, without any form of censorship, the poet says (*Connaissance par les gouffres*, Paris, Gallimard, 1988):

> Such instances of obliteration may be reflected in what is written. If he is able to write, the words he writes will be meaningless to him and to others. He will read them later without understanding them at all, once this coldness of non-thinking, this cloud of veils has passed; they are words he knows but they are about nothing; they appear to have been written entirely at random, even though they are French and correct. They are words that appear only to express the wish

that he wished to say something. He is searching but he does not know what he is searching for.

Such writing is necessarily obscure. In fact, it cannot be read by people who are used to the coldness of reason and clarity; but when it is not being read in such a way (i.e. in accordance with the demands of reason and clarity), it can end up by revealing profound truths, not only about language, but also about the interior world, in which man and things are equal. Writing here becomes an existential motion, the tremor of an earthquake, which starts off by being invisible and becomes visible. It is imbued with nervousness, trembling and physical and spiritual tension, moans and sighs, and intakes of breath; it is despair balanced with hope and hope balanced with despair. The writing infuses the words with nerves, and gives them moans and sighs. They feel as if they are filled with scratches, wounds, destruction and impetuosity. It is a form of writing that does not follow any set or prior path. It is totally opposed to everything that is established. In this respect, it resembles Sufi writing in its non-adherence to the accepted standards, i.e. in its refusal to submit to the accepted norms. This writing makes the norms themselves constantly move and change; they are in a constant state of innovation, as is the writing itself. The norm is itself, like the writing, not fixed but fluid.

6

The crucial point of Rimbaud's experience, which the Surrealists regard as a fundamental source for their theories, is the way he goes beyond the visible to the invisible, something that the Sufis also propose. Novalis says, in this context:

The whole of the visible is incorporated in the invisible and the audible in the inaudible, and the tangible in the intangible. There is no doubt that everything that can be thought about is incorporated into everything that cannot be thought about.

This completely ties in with Rimbaud's production.[6] Bayard believes that Rimbaud has his origins in visionary experience, for he creates an imaginary world; he stirs up a concord of sounds, which include all the possibilities that surround us and which we do not see. He is, as Bayard says, 'a representative and a witness at the same time. He looks in the mirror but he himself is a mirror.'[7]

Bayard says that Rimbaud as visionary knows that the source of the marvellous is intangible and that reality is only an illusion, while he also knows that imagination incorporates and provides another form of reality.

In the letter known as 'the visionary letter', which he wrote on 15 May 1871, Rimbaud describes the relationship between the visible and the unknown or the invisible:

> The poet makes himself *voyant* [seeing] by a long, immense and calculated derailment of all the senses, by a knowledge of all forms of love, suffering and madness. He searches in himself. He exhausts the poison in himself, in order to keep the quintessence. It is unspeakable torture, in which he needs all the faith, all the superhuman strength he can get, by which he becomes the great invalid, the great criminal, the great pariah, above all others – and the supreme Savant! – for he attains the unknown!'

In his comments on this letter, Bayard says that Rimbaud applies what he says in the visionary letter to his poetry, providing glimpses of his tortuous journey through life and making clear his failures, loneliness and despair. 'I am the one who suffers pain and the one who is rebellious [The Just Man].' In *Une Saison en Enfer*, he notes, 'On a particular evening, I made beauty sit on my lap; I saw him bitter, and I insulted him.'

In 'Alchimie de Verbe' in *Une Saison en Enfer*, Bayard says that Rimbaud is writing about his spiritual quest and his liberation by poetry, which become his path to knowledge and the questioning of all human possibilities:

> I wish to discover all secrets, the mysteries of religion, nature, death and birth, the future and the past, the formation of the universe, non-existence. I am a teacher in creating the extraordinary. Listen!

He says that Rimbaud's visionary inspiration allows him to attain knowledge, unlocking the doors to the unconscious; owing to this initiative journey, the poet acquires natural symbolism and is in constant contact with what lies beyond nature, with everything that is said and created. He is captivated by the 'limitless permanence', as Milosz expresses it. Rimbaud is, in fact, a constant seeker after oneness, after the internal structure – the absolute structure, which Raymond Abellio discusses. When talking about imagery, he says, 'This material world is nothing more than a means of summoning up beautiful impressions. It will not reproduce things.'

This oneness, which Rimbaud is searching for, is what the Sufis have been seeking in their own way. It means that the universe is not composed of inanimate and animate matter nor is it composed of two completely contradictory worlds, that of human beings and living creatures and that of inanimate objects, but that it is one world: oneness in a single living presence, in which there is no distinction between death and life. Death is neither a contradiction of life nor an interruption of it. Death in fact becomes the other face of life, another kind of life in this oneness, and in its universal presence.

This oneness is what Breton calls 'the supreme point'.

7

Let us look at how the Sufis regard vision through the words of al-Qushayri (*Letter of al-Qushayri*, p. 176).

> Visions are ideas, which pour into the heart as well as imaginary states, which appear in illusion; if sleep doesn't drown all elements of feelings, the person imagines, when he awakes, that he has really seen something in reality, but it is just his imagination and fantasy. When apparent perception ceases, such illusions are not governed by feeling and necessity, and so the person has a strong sense that he has actually seen something. But when he wakes up and acquires the necessary knowledge, his sense of what he has imagined and his feelings about what he has seen diminish and grow weak. He is like someone who is sitting in heavy darkness, which is lit by the light of a lamp; when the sun rises, it will overcome the lamp's light, so it will appear dim, and at the same time, the sun's light will also diminish. Someone who is asleep is like someone who is lit by a lamp, and someone who is awake is like someone who shuts his eyes against the day, for the person who is awake remembers what he has seen while he was in the state of sleep. Conversations and ideas that come to his heart while he is asleep have many sources. They may come from Satan or from hallucinations of the soul or from ideas from angels and sometimes they may come from the will of God, the most high and mighty, who creates such states in the heart initially ...

I do not want to enter into a detailed analysis of this explanation here. It is sufficient to point out that al-Qushayri, like Surrealists and Rimbaud, regards vision as illuminating knowledge and separate from reason. Sufis add that illumination comes from the heart, and the heart is the tool for knowing concealed knowledge, in a clear and certain way, or the hidden power, which makes known divine truths, or 'mysteries', as Rimbaud calls them. Once man attains this knowledge, he is called the knower; he sees the truth (God, meaning) in all that is revealed and worships it in every image. The knower is the perfect man, who combines the quiddities of being in himself, and in this way becomes a perfect image of the truth. His heart is a mirror, in which his existence is reflected, which is itself a microcosm of the existence of the truth. Thus the knower sees the truth (God), and his heart embraces it. The heart in particular is altered in image and takes on all forms, according to the Sufis. The Sufis cite Qur'anic verses, which point to the heart as both the centre of understanding and the seat of faith.[8]

In the light of what has gone before, we can see that the Surrealist experience including that of Rimbaud is not so much strange as mystical (Sufi) in the way it sets out to discover the world and its secrets. Like the Sufis, the Surrealists use intuition and the way of life as a source of illumination, in their pursuit of knowledge, as opposed to rational and logical methods and in contravention of them. They regard reason as a shackle that only controls them by enchaining them.

We can also see that for both the Sufis and the Surrealists, the dream does not lie completely outside reality, nor is it estranged from it. Dream and reality are, in fact, two sides of the same truth; they incorporate the visible and the invisible.

We can also see that both Sufis and Surrealists regard writing as an experience that connects the visible to the invisible.

Such unprocessed and unrestrained thought and the rays of brightness it conceals led to an outpouring (of creativity) in Sufism and Surrealism, the like of which, according to al-Ghazali, 'No ear has heard, nor eye seen', or, as al-Niffari says, 'cannot be expressed in words'. As words are neither discussed nor censored they flood out like the movement of existence. They contain the basis for visionary thought and writing. If it is true that the movement of existence can be compared to an unending river and horizon, then its transformations are like revelations. Inasmuch as there is no end to revelations, there is no end to the images and knowledge that they contain.

When looked at normally and without being in a state of ecstasy or illumination, things are separate from each other, distinguished by their own characteristics, which make them distinctive and give them meaning. Water is water, fire is fire, and a stone is different from the tree.

But when someone is in a state of illumination, the specifics vanish, the distinguishing marks dissolve. Things cease to be multiple or individual at the moment of illumination, and that is because at that instant their individual essence dissolves. So if the knower in ecstasy ceases to exist as the individual I, so do things cease to exist in their multiplicity or individuality.

At such a moment of illumination, what broad visions open up in front of Rimbaud, for example, when he says, 'I see a mosque in place of a lake' or 'I am thought'. This illuminated vision is the true vision of things.

This also explains how the esotericists have come to reject inspired writing; they say they do not understand it and that it is heretical. This is because they see the manifest in existence only. They say that the Absolute (Being) in essence has a separate existence from the world and that the only thing that links God to man and the universe is creation and control. The esotericists refuse such a separation. They see the Absolute (God) as existing in the world and its objects, and the world and its objects as existing in God. They see existence as creator and created, one and many at one at the same time.

This harmony between the Absolute and things, between the inner (secrets) of existence and the manifest, between the conscious and the unconscious is what broadens the limits of awareness and knowledge. This harmony is realized through illumination, and, because of that, knowledge gained through illumination is the highest form of knowledge.

A vision is explained as the illuminative force, which links seeing with the physical eye (*basra*) to inner perception (*basira*), as Abd al-Qadir al-Jilani points out. A man came to him who claimed to have seen God with his own eyes, and he scolded him and forbade him from speaking in such a way. Then he was asked, 'Is this man lying or telling the truth?' and he replied, 'He is telling the truth, but has gone about it wrongly. He witnessed the light of beauty [God] with his sense of inner perception, and then God pierced through this inner perception to his physical eyes. His physical eyes saw the inner perception. Thus, he thought that his physical eyes saw what his inner perception saw, but in fact he truly saw only his inner perception.'

Ahmed bin Muhammad bin Ajiba al-Hassani explains it in the following way:

> When the spirit is veiled with human form, sight is just one of the senses and the eye can see only tangible objects. But when the human form is possessed by spirituality, sight reflects this sense of inner perception, and he can see only what is seen through inner perception. (*Ikaz al Himam fi Sharh al-Hikam,* and in its margin *al-Futuhat al-Ilahiya fi Sharh al-Mubahith al-Asliya,* Egypt, no date, p. 168.)

The Sufis determine that this relationship between the Absolute and his revelations is the same as that between his essence and his life.

It is said that a man knocked on the door of Abu Yazid al-Bastami's house and he asked him: 'What do you want?'

And he said, 'Abu Yazid.'

And he replied, 'Abu Yazid is not at home.'

It was said that a man said to al-Shibli, 'Where is al-Shibli?'

And he replied, 'He has died, may God not have mercy upon him.'

It is said that Dhu al-Nun al-Masri sent a man to Bastam to find out the circumstances of Abu Yazid al-Bastami and when the man arrived, he went to find him in the mosque and greeted him and Abu Yazid asked: 'What do you want?'

'Abu Yazid,' he replied.

And Abu Yazid said, 'Where is Abu Yazid? I am also looking for Abu Yazid.'

And the man said to himself, 'This man is mad. I have wasted my journey.'

When he returned to Dhu al-Nun and described what he had seen and heard, Dhu al-Nun cried out, saying, 'My brother Abu Yazid has gone among those who have gone to God the most high, the almighty.' (al-Qushayri, p. 52)

An unknown source describes this relationship as follows: 'If I know how I exist, I do not exist and I do not exist if I know how I do not exist (ibid.).

It is as if Sufism is a constant journey of man outside himself or a power that expels man from himself, as Breton says on the topic of self-analysis (*Nadja*, in André Breton, *Œuvres complètes*, Paris, Gallimard, 1988, p. 653).

It is possible to say, in other senses, that man's talents and abilities are not bound by his individuality. The absolute (being, the absent, etc) makes clear its essence through man and his actions, that is, through the domain of the unconscious, and what lies beyond existence exists in existence itself (*Œuvres*, p. 743).

## 8

Ibn 'Arabi describes this Sufi concept of gnosis as follows (*al-Futuhat*, Cairo, Othman Yahya, 1972, pp. 139–46):

> When knowledge is expressed easily, and is nice and easy to understand, then it is the knowledge of theoretical reason … The knowledge of mysteries is hard and difficult to understand when it is put into words and may be rejected by weak and orthodox minds … The knowledge of states lies midway between the knowledge of mysteries and

rational knowledge and most of those who believe in the knowledge of states are people who have been through the Sufi experience; the knowledge of states is closer to the knowledge of mysteries than to rational knowledge ... It is necessary for those who have witnessed it ... Reason does not enter the knowledge of mysteries because it is not on the same level ... The knowledge of states can be experienced only through taste. The man of reason is unable to define it or take issue with it on grounds of proof, as just knowing about the sweetness of honey, the bitterness of aloes and the deliciousness of sex, passion and ardour and desire is insufficient ... It is impossible for someone to learn these forms of knowledge without describing and experiencing them ... The knowledge of mysteries is the knowledge of what lies beyond the boundaries of reason; this knowledge is the sacred spittle of the soul, which the saints and prophets possess in particular ... the man who is blessed with this knowledge knows everything ... there is nothing more noble than this all-encompassing knowledge, which comprehends all other knowledge.

Ibn 'Arabi analyses the universe of this unending gnosis as follows:

The message contained in prophecy continues among people until the day of resurrection. The divine commandments may stop, because they are part of prophecy, but the news of God and his epiphany will never cease or disappear from the world, because if it ceases, nothing will remain to nourish the world and enable it to exist. (*al-Futuhat*, p. 420:12)

Those who believe in illumination name the voice of everything from the inert and plants and animals according to what they hear in the real world and not in imagination, as they hear the speech of ordinary people and the voice from its source, as there is no such thing as silence in existence, because everything in existence speaks the praises of God, and there are no speakers in existence according to us because every essence apart from God is silent and has no ability to speak. But because all these things are phenomena so the speech refers to the phenomenon. (ibid., p. 324:92)

As for general prophecy, its parts are not restricted, and its number cannot be counted, and it is not temporary. It is unceasing, in this world and the next. This is a question that the people of our path have disregarded. I do not know if they have intended to do that or if God has not allowed them to do that, or if they mentioned that and it has not reached us. (ibid., p. 423)

There is no end to knowledge in that the Absolute (God) never reveals himself more than once in the same form, nor does he reveal himself to two people in the same form (ibid., p. 143:10). For God is constantly revealing himself; time places no restraints on his revelations (ibid., p. 334).

This is interpreted as the universe of the heart, the inner place of knowledge, which is being transformed. The heart also transforms itself into endless forms and that is because it conforms to constant existing divine revelations and their rays. The heart is large enough to contain the Absolute and it reflects moment by moment the forms in which the Absolute reveals itself. This reflection is the transformation. As there is no end to revelation, so there is no end to transformation and no end to knowledge. The heart accumulates the attributes of existence.

On this level of congruence between revelation and transformation, the heart dissolves into the Absolute. The knower becomes the Absolute, speaks in his name and is able to say, 'I am not the speaker. I am the Absolute.'

As the manifestations of the Absolute are not cut short and its essence is not repeated, the heart of the knower is created anew at every instant. This also applies to the created world (existence). The world we see at this moment in front of us is not the same world we saw the instant before. The world we will see in the next instant will also be different from the one we have just seen. And what is true for the world is true for the heart of the knower and for man. There is no fixed quiddity. The world is constantly changing, whether it is inert or alive. Truly we do not cross the river twice, as Heraclitus says. The world and mankind change as fast as a breath, as one Sufi said.

This is the theory of continuous creation or new creation, which is consistently present in Arab Sufism. It also exists in the Japanese Buddhist religion, of which Master Dogen (1200–1253) is an exemplar.

Nothing is anything more than a succession of temporary existences, a chain of moments of existence. Everything is born to disappear immediately and then be born again. The world is being reborn at every moment. According to the Buddhists, the world is ephemeral and everlasting at the same time, permanently evanescent and evanescently permanent.

The green mountain is perpetually moving, says Master Kai (1046–1117) in a reference to the mountain of Tai Yo. As it appears to the normal eye, the mountain appears immovable. But when seen extraordinarily, it moves unceasingly, in the sense that it appears and disappears at every moment. In this continuous process of appearing/disappearing, Dogen sees the actualization of the temporal dimension. In order to support this thesis, Dogen relies on the relationship between time and existence. For him existence is nothing more than a brief flash. Time is completely identified with existence. Time is not a kind of place where things exist or events happen, nor is it a shape of an instinctive knowledge. Time is existence itself (Izutsu, *The Concept of Perpetual Creation …*, p. 93). Therefore a sample of time is a sample of existence. The moment is the most infinitesimal fraction of time, which should be seen as an existential instant. What we call things are no more than a chain of ontological instants. This means that nothing remains for two instants, and in every instant the thing renews itself (it is born and it dies). The thing in that instant is completely 'cut off' from what it was in the preceding instant and what it will be in the following instant (ibid., p. 95).

It is satisfying to look at the linguistic-existential relationship that exists between two verbs, *uzila* (to suffer from famine) and *azala* (to become narrow/poor), providing that we look at the language in its natural state, devoid of any religious context. Thus we see that the meaning (the Absent, God, the Absolute, the High Point) has no limit. When man speaks about God, he is not speaking about his essence, but only about the way God manifests himself to him, that is, the image in which he appears. This image comes from man rather than from God. He does not appear in the same image to everyone but rather in a different image to every human being to whom he reveals himself. His manifestations are different, both in clarity and obscurity, according to the difference in the persons. Mankind does not know the essence of God, but knows only an image of him and an interpretation on which he constructs this image.

It is possible to draw comparisons between the way meaning relates to image and meaning to word (verbal expression). Two different words can have two different meanings, such as *thahaba* (go) and *jalasa* (sit); two different words can have the same meaning, such as *thahaba* (go) and *indalaqa* (set off); and two similar words can have two entirely different meanings, such as *wajadtu*, which can mean 'I found it', as when something is missing, or 'I want something passionately', as when one is passionately in love.[11]

It is also possible to make comparisons between the name and the thing named (Abu al-Ala Afifi, 'Ibn 'Arabi in My Studies', included in *al-Kitab al-tadhkari Muhyiddin Ibn Arabi*, Cairo, 1969, pp. 27–28): the name is the outward appearance and the thing named is the inner meaning. The duality of the manifest and the concealed do not point to two different existences but to one existence only, which is made apparent through two expressions. That is apparent, in part from the essence, the truth, and in part from its attributes and names (what has been revealed), the creation.

The meaning (the Absolute) is essentially different from the image that is revealed through it, but it is this image that is knowledge. It is the image and not the image at the same time. It is as knowledge always different from what it is. This does not mean that it is transforming itself and changing according to the diktats of time. The Absolute essentially rejects time, while accepting it through revelation. It remains outside it while it penetrates it.

Time is the time that has been revealed. Time is the time when man sees the image of the revelation. It is the period in which he sees the Absolute through his revelations. The Absolute in its essence has no time. For that reason it has no history.

When man says that he has seen him (the Absolute), this means that he has seen him like a flash. Man can see this flash only through a fog and, in the same way, he can see the Absolute only through an image.

But how does the Absolute become part of something that is other than itself and yet remain itself? The answer to this is that it does not become part of something else but rather that the other manifestation is a part of itself, is itself. The goal of the Absolute in revealing itself in existing forms is not to light up existence so much as to light up the absent and unknown. But it is revelation that allows the setting up of an order of correspondences that place man on the path of mysteries and guide him to the keys that will open them.

In this relationship between the absolute and its revelation it is not possible to shed light upon the secret of poetic language since this language must be elliptical and thus it must be obscure. For this is the other image of this relationship between the visible and the invisible; it is not only the image of the visible but it is also the image of the invisible.

I will end by saying that the Surrealists, like the Sufis, regard knowledge as a tool that enables them to set themselves free from the shackles that enchain man and stand in the way of his complete freedom, and that is because knowledge of the self and existence is true knowledge and because life is on the level of this knowledge and in conformity with it.

According to that, this experience is a living and written practice, which enables them achieve this freedom. Mankind contains an extraordinary inner strength, which is restrained by these chains and, when he discovers this strength, he will be able to achieve his freedom. Surrealism as a form of art merely unveils this strength and gives expression to it.

To put it another way, it is possible to say, in Sufi terminology, that the Surrealists see the immediate manifest existence, in social and cultural terms, as a vast prison, from which it is man's primary duty to escape to a free world in which the inner existence will open up to him.

Thus Surrealism criticizes reality in an analysis that reveals the foundations on which it depends and the organizations through and in which it reveals itself. And as the Sufis work to go beyond *shari'a* and orthodox religion in order to arrive at the truth, the Surrealists work on going beyond the social, cultural and moral establishment, to make man disappear, to enable him to discover his true essence and true existence and true life.

The goal in both cases is to go beyond the prepared system that has gone before and to create a new world or higher reality or 'discover systematically the deepest essence'.

The outward manifestation of this jump is shown in the way it criticizes the established bodies, which make or organize the chains that bind mankind: religion and rationalism (reason and logic) – religion as Church for the Surrealists (*shari'a* for the Sufis) and rationalism as it is revealed through technology and mechanics (veilings and limitations according to the Sufis). For the truth lies elsewhere.

# Imagination

Water is the first transformation of fire.

*Heraclitus*

1

Between the known and the unknown worlds lies what Ibn 'Arabi calls *barzakh* (the intermediate world). This intermediate state also exists between existence and nothingness, for example, or between truth (God) and creation, when perfect man represents *barzakh*. When he appears with divine attributes, he is truth and when he appears with a likeness, he is a creation. *Barzakh*, to put it another way, is the site in which things are transformed, i.e. the site of images and revelations.

Universal truth, according to Ibn 'Arabi, consists of three stages, the highest being that of abstractive or intellectual faculties, the lowest that of feelings and senses; in between the two is an intermediate stage, which combines and links these two stages and which is rational and sensory at the same time. This is the stage of imagination and fantasy.

There are three forms of perception, according to this theory: perception of absolute divine existence, perception of non-existence of the absolute and perception of imaginary existence, which is the intermediary stage between existence and non-existence and the domicile of possibilities, which are infinite.

2

What is imagination, then?

Ibn 'Arabi's answer to that is that in the beginning absolute imagination exists, which is known as the dark mist (*ama*), and by which he means the universal presence and comprehensive order. It accepts images of beings and representations of beings that do not yet exist. All potentialities appear in the dark mist, made euphoric by the breath of God, as Ibn 'Arabi describes it. He refers to the following *hadith* in this context. The Prophet was asked, 'Where was God before creation?' And the Prophet replied, 'He was in the state of *ama*, a dark cloud or state, above which there was emptiness and below which there was emptiness.'

This dark mist is the intermediary world between meaning and its embodiments.

The intermediate state is no more than a shadow of the Absolute. The divine revelations, i.e. the created world, are only shadows of this shadow; things that are perceptible through the senses are shadows of the created world, as perceived through sensory perception. Using the word 'shadow' here signifies cessation, which distinguishes it from existence, which does not cease and which is the permanent Absolute. This shadow is the manifestation or it is the image whose form is represented in divine knowledge before the creation of creation, so the world, according to Ibn 'Arabi, appears in the image of God (Truth).

Existence in relation to this image is like a cloth, i.e. it is a shadow, which is changing, vanishing.

3

If we look at the world, through this existence – this cloth, this occurring existence – the world consists of two worlds, according to Ibn 'Arabi, and the state consists of two states: the world of the absent or the world of *Malakut* (sovereignty/God), to which belongs the state of the absent, and the world of presences or the world of the universe to which the state of witnessing belongs.

The first world is the world of true meaning, which is the world of reason, and the second is the world of literal representation and the senses. We know the first world through inner understanding and the second through the naked eye.

Between the two worlds is a third, which is born out of their conjunction. This is the world of *al-jabrut* (potency). It is at the same time the world of imagination and the state of imagination.

In this third intermediate world, meanings take on images. Meanings here are also intermediate. It is not the world of the absent because the meanings are apparent in images, nor is it a world that can be witnessed because the appearance of meaning through images is an accidental matter in relation to those who see them and not essential to their meaning.

In addition, the state of imagination is the largest of the states, because it brings together the two worlds and is, as Ibn 'Arabi says, the confluence of two seas: the sea of the abstract and the sea of the senses. Imagination comes from the seer and belongs to him and does not come from the thing that is being looked at, nor does it belong to it. The latter is permanent, unchanging. Only its images change and vary unendingly. The first permanence is the permanence of identity, the second permanence, that of change and variability.

Thus, according to Ibn 'Arabi, imagination is the largest of beings and the most perfect of created things, although it is in constant motion, existing-non-existing, known-unknown, negative-positive at the same time. Let us take an example. Look at your image in the mirror: you know it, truly, but you also do not know it truly. This is because senses are wrong and misleading. Your image here is an intermediate stage between the you that you see with your eyes and the you that you see with your sense of inner understanding.

4

Ibn 'Arabi explains that he describes imagination as the most all-encompassing state because God himself, who does not accept images, reveals himself in images in the state of imagination. While his (actual) appearance is impossible, he agrees to appear in this state. To put it another way, imagination is unique among created things, in that it accepts an image of God (truth). Thus we should not be astonished, for example, when the body, in the state of imagination, is seen in two places, something that is rationally impossible. Imagination makes conceivable what reason regards as inconceivable.

Accordingly, imagination is a gauge of how knowledgeable a person is. Ibn 'Arabi emphasizes that someone who is unaware of imagination and its stages does not have the slightest sense of knowledge. The understanding of imaginative revelation is something that particularly belongs to those who are closest to the image of God (*ahl Allahi*).

It is in the nature of this revelation that things that are perceived by the senses are themselves only imaginary: you might see them with your eyes but their reality is different from what the eyes see. This means that the quiddity of imagination is constantly changing and manifesting itself in every image, while the truth is unchanging. This confirms that everything apart from God-Truth is an ephemeral shadow.

This transmutation is the intelligibility of imagination. The world itself is imaginary as it is revealed or made manifest. Created existence is no more than imagination made manifest, according to Ibn 'Arabi.

5

Ibn 'Arabi goes on to say that divine power as it has been brought into being has no greater form of existence than imagination. It is the presence of divine revelation. The creation of the world of imagination is one of the mysteries of the divine name – it was created to make manifest the union between the two opposites. For such a union is impossible through feeling or rationality, but it is not impossible with imagination. Thus, imagination is closest in meaning to the Truth because Truth is the first and the last, the manifest and the concealed, and imagination is its supreme image. What is inconceivable in existence exists in imagination. Imagination is likewise a quiddity of mankind. Through the state of imagination, God is with man in everything he wishes for. According to Ibn 'Arabi, God is, in fact, subject to man's desires, just as man is subject to the wishes of God, in what he wishes for. It is in God's nature to watch over man in order to create for him what he wants in this state, in this world and in the next. Man for his part is subject to God in the images of revelation, for God does not reveal himself in an image except that man is transformed by it. Man is transformed in the images in order to transform God. God is transformed through creation to transform man in this world and the next. Man has a multiplicity of external forms in the next world, as he has various concealed forms in this world, through the image of divine revelation. This is the divine and imaginary correspondence, which is manifest in the other world and concealed in this.

6

Ibn 'Arabi compares imagination to a land in which there are endless marvels and strange things, and where things are found that are inconceivable rationally. He calls this world the theatre of the eyes of the knowers. In this earth, there is a world in the image of mankind; if the knower catches sight of it, he will see himself in it. One of the particular features of this earth is that the knower who has received the revelation is not satisfied with witnessing the revelation, but brings vision and words to it as well. In this world, reason is certainly limited; it is possible to bring together two opposites and for a body to be in two places at once; it is possible for an image to stand on its own and a meaning to stand on its own.

Imagination can create everything except itself, as God can create everything except himself. Thus, it is the most truthful of the created things and the most deserving of the name of perfect man.

Imagination, according to Ibn 'Arabi, is a womb in which the creator creates what he wishes. It is unceasing imagination and it is divine revelation in images that the eye can perceive. As for imagination, which is separate, that is the Absolute, that is the obscurity in which the essence of God dwells.

Although God appears only in an image, he does not reveal himself in the same image twice nor does he reveal himself in the same image to two people, which means that his revelations are never repeated and his image is constantly new. Since imagination imagines what reason denies can be imagined or depicted, it is all-encompassing, as Ibn 'Arabi has described. However, it is simultaneously restrictive, because it is unable to accept feelings and meanings except in imaginative form. For this reason sense is the closest state to it, and it takes its images from feeling.

7

Ibn 'Arabi describes imagination as rays of light, which are unlike any other light. They understand divine revelations. Imagination is not iniquitous. Rather, it is truthful and contains nothing base. Imagination understands with its light what it understands, and it does not commit faults. Errors always come from reason, i.e. from judgment. Imagination does not judge. Imagination understands through its sense of imagination rather than its sense of perception, although the visual sense is what gives awareness to both of them. The secret of that is that man understands both imaginary images and images that can be perceived through the senses through his sense of imagination. However, things that are perceptible through the senses do not have different forms and are not seen in different places in the same form. Confusing imagination with the senses is a specious argument, according to Ibn 'Arabi; in fact it is the worst form of sophistry.

Ibn 'Arabi elucidates the relationship between imagination and other human powers by saying that the perfect man, who is the intermediary between Truth (God) and the world, has three stages: the stages of reason and feeling and the third intermediate state between them, which is imagination.

Each sensory power has two aspects: the aspect, which is turned towards things that are perceptible through the senses in the evidential world and the aspect turned towards imagined things in the state of imagination. This state is larger than the evidential world.

Imagination draws on what the senses understand and stores it in its treasury, and the faculty that composes images utilizes this as its subject matter and it is this that goes into the composition of images: they will be strange and unknown images made from parts that are known and familiar.

The faculty of recollection retains these images and it has two gatekeepers. The first of them is memory, which retains abstract meaning, and the second is imagination, which retains the image. The faculty of memory fixes the meaning.

As for thought, it is a faculty that serves the faculty of reason; and thought can be found only in the imaginative faculty, for it is a place that brings together what the faculty of the senses provides. Reason does not accept anything apart from what it has learnt through the perceptive faculty or what thought has given it. It witnesses the meanings, stripped bare from the material, that the imagination raises. Reason is connected to the senses through imagination, in other words: reason takes from thought, which takes from imagination, which takes from the senses. Thus Ibn 'Arabi describes reason as a poor thing, which knows nothing apart from what it receives from this faculty (imagination). As for seeing by itself, it knows nothing apart from the necessities with which it was endowed.

Both illusion and reason are forces of control in man, but illusion is more powerful than reason, except that it quickly disappears because it is not bound by anything; this is the opposite of reason, which is chained by what it has gained. Because of that, the effects of illusion on the self are stronger than the effects of reason so the control of illusion is the more powerful on mankind.

8

To summarize, there is constant and separate imagination. Separate imagination is the presence of complete and universal *barzakh*, in which imaginative correspondences and intermingling exist. In this presence, God is revealed, the spirits of angels appear and meanings descend in images and sensory moulds. Everything that appears in the separate imaginative state is an incarnation, not an embodiment, and cannot be distinguished except through divine power, which God gives to those whom he chooses.

As for constant imagination, it is the imaginative creative faculty in man by which he enters the state of separate imagination in wakefulness and sleep.

Thus imagination has two states, the state of constancy and the state of separateness. The state of constancy vanishes when what is imagined disappears, while the state of separateness is a particular state that can always receive spiritual meanings and spirits.

9

Man likewise has two states, the state of wakefulness and the state of sleep. What he sees in wakefulness is seeing, and what he sees in sleep is vision/dream. Perhaps some people perceive in wakefulness what they perceive in sleep, and that is rare and special.

Sleep is a state that transports man from the world of the senses to the *barzakh* or intermediate stage. When a man sleeps, the eye in his face looks at the world of imagination, which is the most complete of worlds and the source of the world; it has true existence and control over all matters; it embodies meaning and makes what is not visible in itself visible in itself, and provides images for what does not have an image, and makes the impossible possible.

In sleep, it is possible to move from the world of the senses to the internal world, for it discloses what is in the storehouse of imagination. Images can be seen in sleep and it uses the pleasurable states and the speed of changing from one state to another.

Thus imagination shows us that existence is in constant movement and is constantly changing.

10

The spiritual ascent of Muhammad (*mi'raj*) or his nocturnal journey (*isra*) is accomplished through the power of imagination. It is a gnostic ascent, which starts with physical things, then proceeds to the obscure essence, then to the state of simple nature, then to the preserved tablet where God lists created things, then to the supreme pen, which holds the knowledge of sovereignty, and then to the world of fierce love, created from a dark mist, and finally to the dark mist, which is the meaning that has been fixed in the essence of possibilities. From this dark mist, the ascent ends in the names of deanthropomorphism and arrives at a state that accepts neither deanthropomorphism nor anthropomorphism, so it places God above limits by denying deanthropomorphism and beyond comparison by denying his anthropomorphism, that is, it disallows qualification.

## 11

What comes to the heart from the higher world is what Ibn 'Arabi calls *waqi'a* (annunciatory vision). *Waqi'a* might come by way of speech or similitude, for it is one of the signs of prophecy. *Waqi'a* is for walis (holy men) as inspiration is for prophets and is called authentic vision, which is one of the parts of prophecy.

*Waqi'a* is the beginning of divine inspiration, as it comes from the essence of man. Some people see such visions while they are asleep. Others see them during *fana'* and others still see them while they are awake, without *waqi'a* veiling them from the perception of their senses.

Vision as part of prophecy comes from God and is the start of inspiration and occurs only in a state of sleep. Inspiration starts with vision, not with sense, because rational meanings are closer to imagination than they are to sense, for senses are from a lower plane and meaning is from a higher plane, and imagination comes between them. Inspiration is meaning. Because of that, inspiration begins with the descent of abstract rational meanings in sensory moulds fixed in the state of imagination, in sleep or in wakefulness, and it comes from what is perceived by the senses in the presence of things perceptible through the senses. If meaning wants to descend to the feeling then it must pass through the state of imagination before it can reach the feelings. It is one of the facts about imagination that it imagines everything that it obtains in the image of things perceptible by the senses. For if this divine inspiration arrives in a state of sleep it is called a vision, and if it arrives in a state of wakefulness, it is called imagination. Thus prophetic inspiration begins with imagination.

## 12

Imagination is not wanted for itself but rather for the effect it will have on sensory existence, which will demonstrate its effect on the senses. Explaining imagination means transporting it or taking it across to another imagination, where the listener will imagine it to the extent of his understanding. The first imagination might correspond with the second imagination (the imagination of the writer and the imagination of the reader, for example, or the imagination of the listener and the imagination of the speaker) or it might not correspond; in the first instance, the correspondence is called understanding.

Vision does not make mistakes, and every vision is true, but the person who translates it may make a mistake in the interpretation of it. Therefore, only God and people he has chosen from among the prophets or special saints know the status of the world of imagination.

Ibn 'Arabi believes that the dream, which comes suddenly without any preparation or prior thought, is closer to the truth. This is because imagination that is linked to consciousness is less rich than imagination that is linked to unconsciousness.

> For he who interprets non-vision is interpreting something he has imagined by himself and which he has conjured up from the start, and makes it seem as if he has seen it by his senses, and he is weaker than someone who has expressed something from imagination without thinking about it in advance and without conjuring it up, like a person who has seen a vision. For imagination in this case shows the seer what it contains, without its being conjured up by him. The person who is awake is not like that, for his imagining is weak because it is clouded by the veils of the senses, so he needs force, and intensifies and doubles his interpretation. It is said, I crossed the river effortlessly, because the river is not something that

has been conjured up or imaginary, but it is present to the senses, as the dream is present in imagination, and has not been conjured up or thought about in advance. Therefore when you have to interpret the dream, the interpreter needs a double amount of imagination in order to convey the symbols of what is symbolized in it. (*al-Futuhat*, p. 454:3)

## 13

Logic freezes the representations of the world into a series of contradictions – the real and the possible, the action and the dream, the normal and the mad – contradictions that constitute the apparel of social conservatism, which is designed to ward off any strange behaviour by the individual. When the Surrealists rejected logic, they no longer had anywhere to take refuge other than by using the means employed by the poets: intuition, inspiration, instinct; and they worked to display their superiority in these methods. (Béhar and Carassou, *Le Surréalisme*, p. 162)

'Imagination is the only thing that works,' according to Aragon.

Nothing, neither strict logic, nor the power of emotions, has the power to make me convinced about reality, or convince me that I am not basing it on a delirium of interpretation. (Aragon, *Paris Peasant*, Paris, Gallimard, 1926, as quoted in Béhar and Carassou, p. 162)

For imagination, which we all possess, is alone able to lift the embargo from the areas that we are unable to enter except through it. It alone has the power to banish 'the phallus of logic'.
Breton says,

What I love best in you, beloved Imagination, is that you are unforgiving … Imagination alone demonstrates what is possible and that is sufficient to halt, if only for a little, the terrible forbidden. (ibid., p. 163)

Thus the Surrealists study the role of imagination, and try to discover its dynamic and its functioning.

They aim at attaining 'uncontrolled thought', which is not subject to sensory awareness or social constraints. They explore a variety of ways of self-discovery to bring this about, which include automatic writing, hypnotic sleep, dreams, fabricated delirium and mental delirium-critical. (ibid., p. 172)

These are all means of taming or gaining control of the body, which are similar to attempts by the Sufis to eliminate the veil that blocks off the world of the self from the real world.

Imagination has a particular significance, according to Sufis and Surrealists, not so much because it is illusory but because it is an unknown being and therefore can become real. Human imagination, according to Nerval, does not invent anything in this world or the other that is not true.

## 14

As for the dream, Maurice Blanchot believes that 'the freedom of writing' in the history of Surrealism 'is linked to experiments with sleep'. In fact, automatic writing did not long remain the sole means of reaching the vast continent that was revealed through it. After 1922, hypnotic sleep had become another means of exploring this obscure land. This form of sleep also eliminated the constraints that blocked thought and instead opened the way to marvels and freedom. Aragon says, 'That beautiful word freedom takes on meaning for the first time at this point: freedom begins when the marvellous begins.'

The practice of hypnotic sleep leads to the abolition of man's self-possession, a confusion of feeling and a state of self-abandonment, which sometimes manifests itself in violent acts. Therefore it puts a stop to the desire for 'primary mental health', as Breton says.

Aragon says about the dream, that since time immemorial it has been seen as a form of inspiration. Gods speak to their victims in dreams, etc. It should be noted that those who carefully note down their dreams today don't intend to set up a relationship with the supernatural. They narrate what they see in the dream with faith and objectivity. The objectivity here is almost complete, in that there is not any kind of censorship that can interfere between the sleeper and reality as it appears between the one who is awake and reality.

In the introduction to the first issue of the *Surrealist Revolution*, he says:

> The dream alone leaves man with his rights to freedom completely intact. Thanks to the dream, death no longer has an obscure meaning, and the meaning of life loses its importance. We are all at the mercy of the dream and it is up to us to bear its authority. It is a frightening tyrant dressed up in mirrors and flashes. What is the paper, the quill or the writing, what is the poem when faced with this giant whose muscles are bound up with the muscles of the clouds?

The Surrealists open up the doors of dreams to all those to whom the night is miserly. Surrealism snaps such chains apart.

This magazine prioritizes the rendition of dreams as a record of what it is impossible to say; dreams become a means of resolving the contradictions in human life, because the dream state and reality are like two isotropic receptacles, which seek their own level: their waters merge into a single entity.

Delirium is linked to the dream state, and Breton believes that there are firm links between the dream and various types of delirious activity, which are present in mental hospitals. The fabrication of mental illness, like the narration of dreams, also permits progress in the revealing of the unconscious or the internal continent. Thus Surrealism re-examines the issue of madness and the procedures that are used, it claims, to define mental illness. It backs people with mental illness against the establishment and detects genius in the insane. (The theologians and theological reasoning regarded Sufism as a kind of madness.)

## 15

If we can overcome reason and logic by using imagination, dream and delirium, then we can overcome reality and attain what lies behind reality or what is described as the absent in Sufi terminology, where the mystery, truth and meaning lie. Thus the dream, as the Surrealists see it, is not a flight from a world that does not satisfy the individual, but rather a spur, which prods him to overcome difficulties and obstacles. Surrealism is the discovery of the inner depths of the self, and it is also the discovery of the external world, not to know it as it is, but rather to recreate it.

But what lies behind reality is not an absolute and separate existence in itself; it is a notion linked to reality, which connects meaning and image in Sufism. What is marvellous and astonishing is how what lies behind reality appears in reality. The significance that the Surrealists attribute to this wondrous marvel leads them to reconsider their position on the external world and move towards a reconciliation between the allegorical and material stance, which they adopt subsequently. Thus they emphasize the image and feeling and desire, rather than logical methods in the practice of knowledge. The Surrealist concept of knowledge has nothing to do with Hegelian rationalism or Marxist action, but it is an act of freedom.

Breton says with reference to the efficacy of the human role, 'Our place in the universe has a character which goes beyond logic and which can only be understood through the similes we see through the theory of correspondences.' He describes this theory as being the seat of occultism, in which, according to him, 'everything is related to an individual whole and has a necessary relationship with every other element of this group', so that it appeared to Breton that at a certain instant, 'the lion is in the box of matches and the box of matches is in the lion'.

Thus the Surrealists substitute the laws of a shared universe and the concept of simile for the laws of causality and the theory of compatibility. From this they attain a clear knowledge of the world.

This sensory and direct knowledge cannot be separated from convulsive beauty, according to Breton, and such beauty as this 'only results from feelings, which take possession of the things that are being revealed, and from a complete certainty provided by the solution, which because of its particular nature doesn't reach us through ordinary logical ways'.

For Surrealism at first repudiates an external reality and then wishes to transform it. In the process Surrealists persist in re-explaining it. Their growing awareness of similes starts increasingly to dictate their stance *vis-à-vis* the world.

From then on, Surrealist research in the field of knowledge is based on finding proximities and likenesses between things and beings. At issue is their ability to receive secret signs, readily and boldly.

At the heart of this world of objects and beings is Paris, which has an overwhelming significance. Paris is the city in which everything becomes possible. Every Surrealist talks about his wanderings in this city, searching for the golden fleece (Aragon in *Paris Peasant*, for example, or Breton in *Nadja*).

Finally, Breton terms the signs of the unknown 'objective chance'. Through the revelations of 'objective chance' and 'automatic writing', the yearning imagination discovers its firm link with external necessity. Each one of us forms inside himself a singular collection of what surrounds him. For the world, according to Breton, 'is a form of symbolic writing whose symbols require a solution'.

Through poetic practice, the Surrealists discover in 'the alchemy of language' the sense of 'the great magical work', which makes the disciple penetrate the mysteries of the universe. This is connected to a desire to transform man and the universe and return man's place to him, by reclaiming his lost powers.

Breton stresses this subject and explains it, saying, 'Scientific knowledge of nature is worthless except by establishing contact with nature, by poetic means and, I hasten to add, by means of myth. It remains clear that every scientific advance achieved within the framework of an incomplete social structure works against man and increases the gravity of this position.'

Remembering the lost paradise allows mankind to reject the conditions imposed upon him in this world and furnishes him with sufficient strength to work to overcome them.

Emphasizing the importance of imagination, the Surrealists ennoble the derangement of the senses or their suspension, which will lead them to a more exalted dimension and take them beyond the purely logical view. They renew the theory of poetic creation by making imagination its fundamental instigator. Giving imagination this role and significance means that they reject the rationalist tendency, which has directed our ideas of the world since ancient times (Bartoli-Anglard, *Le Surréalisme*, p. 65). Breton reflects this notion, when he declares that imagination is a more trustworthy source of knowledge than reason. Jacqueline Chenieux-Gendron explains this, by saying that imagination makes ontological creations out of our creations, because reason is constantly threatened with wrongdoing (ibid., p. 65).

From what I have just said, it can be seen that imagination is an intermediary between the soul, which is from the absent world, and the senses, which are part of this world, and it is a repository from which the faculty of the self extracts its prime matter. Imagination is absolute, and even if it is restrained by things perceptible through the senses, it is not mistaken, because it understands objects through its light, and light does not err. Error comes from judgment, and imagination sees but is not the source of judgment. It creates what it likes as it likes.

The poet tries to attain the unknown, through the faculty of imagination – to see what cannot be seen and to hear what cannot be heard. Whether it is recalling things understood by the senses or imagining new things, imagination is re-forming things in both cases: it brings together the far-flung elements and creates new relationships between them. Imagination does not aim to persuade but rather to create the marvellous and the sweet; it does not aim to produce mere curiosities, but rather to enrich the sensitivity and expand the consciousness, so that the reader will feel that everything before him is beginning again and is taking on a new meaning.

This is what Ibn Sina means when he says that no word that is not imaginary is poetic, even if it is rhythmical and rhyming, that poetry requires imagination in it, and that mere opinions are not sufficient.

There is no intermediary between imagination and the Absolute, according to Ibn 'Arabi, as there is no intermediary between imagination and things perceived by the senses. It is the meeting point. The Absolute descends to it and the things perceived by the senses ascend to it. It is the state in which the Absolute (God) reveals himself to mankind, or it is the state of embodiment.

Ibn 'Arabi speaks about this state in the sense of love. He says that the force of his imagination led to 'my love embodying my beloved, which appeared in front of my eyes, in the same way as Gibril [the archangel Gabriel] appeared in corporeal form to the Prophet. I was not able to look at it and it addressed me and I listened to it and I understood it and it left me for days and I did not swallow food. Every time the table was brought to me it stood beside it and looked at me and said in a language I could hear with my ears. 'Do you eat while seeing me?' So I couldn't eat but I wasn't hungry, for I was replete with looking at it and grew fat and it was like food for me.'

# Love

Love is pleasure and reality is astonishing.
*al-Daqaq*

There is no love between two people
until one of them says to the other: oh, me.
*al-Sirri al-Saqati*

1

What is love?[1] The Sufi answers such a question by saying that love cannot be defined but only understood through experience.

If love is not defined by its essence, it is defined by its consequences, its influence and its manifestations. We must taste love, in order to know it. This taste does not quench our thirst, for love is a drink that leaves one thirsting; anyone who says that love has satisfied his thirst doesn't know what love is. For once a lover has tasted love his thirst increases.

This means that love does not exist in a state of permanence where it can be analysed and defined, but it is constantly moving and changing, to such an extent that it appears non-existent or absent, as Ibn 'Arabi says. Love is the desire to become united with the beloved, not for the sake of the person or to exist by itself but to continue and perpetuate the union.

For continuance and perpetuity are non-existent: that is, they are created continuously, and their term is infinite. Thus love is a state of communion, attached to a being whose existence is constantly beginning. It is as if love is a sense of longing, continuously yearning for a non-existent beloved. In other words, existence is not loved for itself but for what we would like it to be – and this is creation and remains creation, or remains 'non-existent', as Ibn 'Arabi puts it.

Love does not consent to be divided or shared. The heart is unable to love two people. Thus it is one of love's characteristics that, 'it deafens the lover and makes him unable to hear anything except the words of his beloved, it blinds him so that he is unable to see anything except the face of his beloved, and makes him speechless, so that he is unable to talk about anything except for his beloved and the one whom his beloved loves. He sets a seal upon his heart, excluding everything except the love for his beloved; he shoots the bolt on the treasure house of his imagination and imagines nothing but the image of his beloved. Without such signs, it is not love nor is the one who practises it a lover. For the principle of love is that the lover becomes identified with his beloved and loses himself in love, so that he will no longer be himself but dissolved into his beloved.'

Therefore man does not in fact love anyone other than himself, because he loves only himself in the other. No one loves the beloved for the sake of the beloved but only for his own sake. Thus, the lover is subject to the rule of love, not to rule of the beloved.

Ibn 'Arabi says that love is like a sweetness and there is nothing sweeter than it; it has a nectar, which he describes as a constant revelation that never ceases. The heart, rather than the faculties of reason or perception, is the vessel from which love is drunk. For reason is binding – the word is derived from 'uqal (to hobble a camel) – as are feelings. But the heart is in a constant state of flux. As love has many various and contradictory rules, only the heart, which has the power to transform and be transformed by love according to these rules, is able to accept it.

The vessel in the sense of the heart signifies the external appearance, the nectar signifies what is visible in it and the act of drinking is what the revelations reveal to the person receiving them, i.e. the drinker.

The nectar of love can also mean the love God has for us and which makes us love him. For when we love him, we know by experiencing his love for us (by drinking the nectar of his love for us) that his love for himself is the same as his love for us. We are intoxicated with this nectar so that we are no longer aware that we love him, although we feel that we do. This is a gnostic revelation. For a lover can never be a knower and a knower can never be a lover. His love for us intoxicates us out of our love for him. But our love for him does not intoxicate us out of our love for him. This is what distinguishes the lover from the knower, and love from knowledge. Thus, the nectar of his love for us is the knowledge that our love for him comes from his love for us. He makes us unaware of our love for him. For the Sufi is a lover and not a lover, and he does not know what is said about him in intoxication, because those who are intoxicated do not reason.

In this, love is the lover himself and his essence, and is not an attribute of its meaning.

Love has two causes, which are beauty and charity, according to Ibn 'Arabi. Beauty is loved for itself. The world is beautiful in the sense that it is created in the image of God (God is beautiful and he loves beauty). There is no place more beautiful than the world, though he created what he created endlessly. Were it not for the beauty of God, beauty would not have appeared in the world, and were it not for the fineness of created beings, the fineness of the creator would not be known.

The second cause of love is charity. Charity comes only from the creator, and there is no one more charitable than him. If man loves charity, then he loves God.

It can also be said that whoever loves the world for its beauty only loves God, since God has revealed nothing apart from this world, which he has created in his image.

God reveals himself as an example of an image, in the world of representations, as a revelation, which is visible and manifold, in which abstract meaning, forms of knowledge and spirit are embodied in imaginary examples. (Surat al-Baqara and Surat Al-'Amran: 'they will come on the day of judgment, with their tongues and lips, and they will be witness to the people who read them'). If the souls are embodied and represented in corporeal images, they will take on natural properties.

Inasmuch as man is a being, created in the image of God, then he has the state of the universal name. He is like a mirror of God (truth). God manifests himself only as 'beautiful' to man and in man. Thus man is in love with the revelations of God. This might explain the prophet's love of women: 'There are three things that I love in this world: women and perfume and prayer, which is the most pleasurable for me.' Love is 'the greatest and most perfect passion'. Passion is a tool of the soul. Desire ennobles the person who is desired, and abases him as it diminishes. It is the wish to take pleasure in what it should take pleasure. There are two types of pleasure: spiritual and natural. Given that the soul is partially born of nature, for nature is its mother and the divine spirit is its father, spiritual desire will never be rid of its natural component.

Man's pleasure in his perfection is the most pleasurable form of pleasure, and therefore his pleasure in the one in whose image he is made is the most pleasurable form of pleasure as well. The proof of that, according to Ibn 'Arabi, is that, 'pleasure does not course through man's entire being, nor is he completely annihilated at the sight of some thing, nor do love and passion course through his spiritual nature unless he falls in love with a slave girl or a boy. That is because he accepts it with his complete being because it is in his image, while everything apart from that in the world is only a part of him so he accepts it only partially with the suitable part of him. So man is not annihilated by something he loves unless that thing looks like him. If divine revelation falls on the same image as God created Adam in it, then the two will have the same meaning and complete pleasure will result, which will be apparent in every part of man. Therefore those who know the value of women and their secrets cannot abstain from loving them. Loving them completes the knower. It is a legacy from the Prophet according to *hadith*. In that sense, it is divine love because our love for women brings us closer to God.'

Our natural love, our love for women is ignited by a look or a sound. It is possible that the image of the woman whom we have seen or heard corresponds with the image we have of her in our imagination, or it may be greater or smaller than it. The image may become too powerful for the imagination to contain. In such a case, the imagination will become confused, as the image of the imagination merges with the image of the person being imagined. The lover will be distracted and become muddled and bewildered. It will affect him, in the same way as imagination affects perception, as happens when someone fantasizes about falling, and falls as a result.

As we know, the world, when seen from Ibn 'Arabi's perspective, consists of three states: the unseen, the seen and the imaginary. Since the state of imagination is the most beautiful in essence and the most perfect in being, the seer perceives in it 'what it was before its being, and what it was and what it is now'. Imagination is the state that brings things together. In this state, as Ibn 'Arabi says, the lover loves the image of his beloved, which he has conjured up out of his imagination, rather than the beloved herself. He loves what he has made and what he has looked up to, for he loves himself and in the same way celebrates what he has made.

This is what Ibn 'Arabi calls the love of love – being on fire with love for love itself rather than for the beloved.

Perhaps this is why he says that passionate lovers find greater and stronger pleasure in their love of God than in their love of woman and sex. This is because the divine image is more completely represented in man than the image of sex. God can be the eyes and ears of man, but sex does not have the power to do that.

If love is the cause of revelation, then hearing is the cause of the creation of the world. Man's love of God began when he first heard the word of God. The universe knew nothing of God except his word. When it heard him, it took pleasure in listening to him, and was unable not to exist. At the basis of being is the sweetness of speech. Therefore hearing has a natural propensity for agitating and moving and transporting the listener because from the moment when the listener heard the word 'Be!' he was transported and moved from a state of non-being to a state of being and came into existence. Agitation among the people of hearing (the Sufis) and their ecstatic rapture can be attributed to this. The person in ecstasy obtains a knowledge he does not possess through ecstatic rapture, which ennobles and completes his soul. Not every instance of hearing produces ecstatic rapture and ecstatic rapture can exist without hearing. Were it not for speech, the disciple would not be able to make his desires known, and were it not for hearing, we would not be able to understand what has been said to us.

Hearing is divided into three categories: divine, spiritual and natural.

Divine hearing is the hearing of mysteries – from everything, through everything and in everything. It belongs to those for whom God is the ears with which they hear. This hearing is the first stage of being of the universe, and with it the end will be accomplished. The first existence of the universe was brought into being by hearing and its last will be brought to an end by God through hearing. The true knower is in a state of constant hearing.

Spiritual hearing is linked to the divine writings on the tablet of existence, which neither change nor alter. The whole of existence is a parchment spread out, and the world is the writing jotted down upon it. The pen speaks and the intellect listens and the words are inscribed and witnessed. The eye that sees them is the eye that understands them.

Knowledge and gnosis come with spiritual hearing, as a whole and without matter.

As for natural hearing, Ibn 'Arabi says our love of God was brought about by hearing the words of God. The reason why we are moved and placated by the sound of music is because the word 'Be', which originated from the divine image, is a mystery and a proof. 'Ecstatic rapture occurs particularly in people who are listening to music; it comes to them by way of the celestial spheres, and the movement of the spheres has a pleasurable and enjoyable melody.'

Knowledge is not originally associated with natural hearing, but those who possess natural hearing are delighted or saddened at heart when they hear music and speech.

Music and speech originate in divine speech and depend upon it, for it provides a very powerful foundation. This explains its influence on character. It derives its power from the strength of its origins. Therefore no one is able to remain unemotional or be untouched by joy or sadness when he listens to music, specifically when it touches the right heart. It should be pointed out that, in Ibn 'Arabi's opinion, the divine truths from which music is derived are more powerful than those from which speech originates.

Thus the universe in its entirety is based on hearing the word 'Be'.

There are three stages of love: divine love, spiritual love and natural love.

Divine love is personified by man's love for God and God's love for man. Spiritual love is represented by the struggle to please the beloved when the lover no longer has any objective or wish in relation to his beloved. Natural love is personified by the lover seeking to obtain all the objectives of natural love, whether or not they make the beloved happy.

The beloved is not loved in natural love for himself, rather he is loved for what happiness and pleasure he brings. This fact also applies to spiritual and divine love.

The goal of natural love is union so that the spirit of the lover becomes the spirit of his beloved through enjoyment and stimulation of desire.

Love therefore has a mental and physical effect on the lover; Ibn 'Arabi explains this by describing how the imagination of the lover is unable to encompass the image of the beloved as it grows in size and significance. He becomes emaciated as a result, his form changes, he becomes pale, his lips become dry, his eyes become hollow, he grows weak, he swoons when he sees the beloved, is stupefied and finally may go mad.

The lover does not try to explain the actions of the beloved, but accepts and lives with them. Analysis is a rational quality, and the lover does not possess reason. In fact, no good can come of a love that is planned rationally. For love and reason are incompatible. Therefore, the rule of love must oppose the rule of reason. If, as Ibn 'Arabi says, speech is a mark of reason and silence a mark of ardent love, then the relationship between madness and speech is discernible – for madness starts when the lover is no longer able to speak, that is, when speech betrays him. Thus the moment of the brief encounter between madness and speech – between madness, which speaks, and speech, which becomes mad – is the moment of expression, or the moment of poetry par excellence, and it is a rare moment.

In spiritual love, the lover aspires to become like the beloved, at the same time as carrying out his duty towards him and knowing his value. While natural love can be subjected to limitations, measurements and comparisons, spiritual love on the contrary is limitless and cannot be measured or compared to anything. Thus when two lovers are overcome by spiritual love, neither complains about being separated from the other, as they are not part of the physical world and are not restricted and confined by meanings.

In spiritual love, the beloved loves his beloved for the sake of the beloved. It is a universal love, the opposite of natural love, in which the lover loves only for his own sake.

If spiritual love is clothed and made to appear in a natural image, then the essence of the beloved is the same as the essence of the lover and the essence of the lover is the same as the essence of the beloved. The lover can rightfully proclaim: 'I am the one whom I love and the one whom I love is I. I am consumed with passion for no one but myself, I yearn for no other, I love no other. I am dying for myself and I am possessed, for I am the beloved lover, I am the desired desirer.'

Thirdly, divine love is the love of God for man and the love of man for God. In divine love, man sees his being as a manifestation of God, and it is therefore the apparent truth (God), whose inner essence is unseen, like the soul in the body, and never perceived and never witnessed except by the person who loves him. Thus the truth (God) is a manifestation of God to man and he is depicted like a human being with limits and scope and characteristics, and man witnesses this manifestation and at that point becomes the beloved of the truth (God).

For the love of God is that he loves us for himself and for us, while our love for him is called divine love. Our love for him is made up of two forms of love together: spiritual and natural love. 'This is something that is difficult to imagine, because not everyone understands the matters in the same way. Divine love is signified by a love for all engendered things in every presence, whether they are suprasensory, sensory, imaginal or imaginalized, and thus God describes himself as loving the manifestations [of himself], and this love has no end.'

Ibn 'Arabi says there are four states of love:

1. Fancy (*hawin*): This represents the point at which love falls into the lover's heart and is derived from the word *hawa*, meaning to fall. It is powerful, as it comes from the supreme world. In this state, the lover loses his will in the beloved.

    If the state of *hawa* did not exist, then no lover would fall in love, as Ibn 'Arabi says, since man is tested by it to see whether he drops or rises, and is saved or mourns.

2. Love (*hub*): This is sincerity of fancy in the heart, and it is purity from all dirt. The power of this love is so great that nothing can eliminate it.

3. Passion (*'ashq*) is an excess of love. It lights the flame of longing and ecstatic rapture. *'Ashq* coils itself around the lover until it is completely intertwined with him. It is derived from *'ashaqa*, meaning the tendrils of ivy, which wind themselves about what is growing near them. In the state of *'ashq*, the lover is dominated by the beloved.

In *'ashq* for man or God, the lover merges completely with the beloved (either man or God) so that nothing remains. His external self is captivated by the beloved's external self, and his concealed self is captivated by the beloved's concealed self.

Love is not called *'ashq* unless it appears at the very centre of the lover's heart, and occupies him completely, and blinds him to everything apart from his beloved. His love courses through his entire body and his strength and his spirit. It flows through his veins like blood, and floods his joints, and embraces every part of his body, physically and mentally, so there is no space left in him for anything else. His speech and his hearing are subsumed in love, and he sees love in everything and in every image.

4. Affection: This is the abiding quality of fancy, love or passion in the way it grieves and pleases without distinction.

2

Since divine theophanies exist in forms that are closely associated with change, then the influence of the theophanies arouses various emotions in the lover, such as grief, ecstatic rapture, sadness, torment, intoxication and passion, as well as longing, ardent desire, passionate love, adoration, weeping, weakness, broken-heartedness, torment and burning desire. An excess of love eliminates reason, causes emaciation, ceaseless thinking, intrinsic anguish and anxiety, sleeplessness, distraction and imbecility.

Ibn 'Arabi is acquainted with some of these emotions; he says ardent desire, for example, exhausts the beloved because of its heartsick tenacity. Love has no quality that is more all-encompassing than ardent desire (*ghiram*).

He says heartsickness (*kamad*) causes the lover to melt, and is the most grievous sadness of the heart. The sufferer does not shed tears but moans and groans instead.

He says torment is a fire that blazes up and reclaims the hearts of the lovers, burning everything it finds there except the lover.

He says that burning desire is the flame of desire, and passion is the expansive stage of love because it is derived from air.

He says distraction is preoccupation with love rather than the beloved, and intoxication is an abandonment of reason and the fourth stage of love – the first stage being tasting, the next drinking, the third, quenching the final, intoxication.

Then he says passionate love is a passion for beauty and confusion brought on by coquetry; the lover's heart is in flux and he is bewildered in the changing of his heart.

He says sadness is the most difficult manifestation of love and the hardest to bear. He says mad love is intoxication of reason and cannot be ordered, and grief comes about because of the diverse cares caused by the multiplicity of images in which his beloved reveals herself to him. He says passionate ardour is what happens to the heart when the states eliminate it, and torment is the raging thirst, the fire and burning desire that the lover experiences.

And he says that love blinds and deafens.

3

It is possible to say, based on the above, that woman, in the sense of the beloved, symbolizes creative femininity, the womb of the universe. In that sense, she is the mother of existence, the place in which being is. In order to be present in her, the lover must be absent from himself, from his qualities. He must make his qualities disappear in order to confirm the essence of his beloved and to exist in this essence. He will continue to be veiled from her, if his qualities persist. So he will remain in opposition to himself as long as his qualities persist. When his qualities cease, when he dies, he lives.

Just as created beings have no existence outside of God, in the sense that if 'the pre-existent essence does not exist in the newly created tangible and reasonable, then it will be non-existent' (Ibn Khaldun), since, in reality, there is no existence except in the eternally pre-existent, then, in the same way the lover does not exist except through what he loves.

However, death in Sufism is a means to a higher life, just as death in love is a means of delivering oneself from the limitations of the human body. 'Love is a torture. Love kills,' says Jallal al-Din al-Rumi. In death the soul is delivered from its individuality and becomes plural. Through love the self goes out to the other. Individuality is a wall between the I and the other. Thirst for repletion, for full existence, drives the ardent Sufi lover to death, which he must pass through in order to be transported from the part to the whole, in order to be transported to life. 'Kill me, my trusted followers as in my death is my life,' says al-Hallaj.

For death alone can put an end to dualism. For there is no unity at this level without death. Life is incomplete if you do not die. The Sufi lover dies for life, because of life.

This explains the intense connection between sex and religion, on the one hand, and death, on the other. This connection is represented in delirium and ecstasy. It is a form of death and resurrection at the same time. What is extinguished dies and what is resurrected remains. The non-essential dies and the essential remains. Love is ecstasy; life is resurrection from death. Ecstasy rescues the lover from external form and appearance, and makes him a diaphanous being, a pure essence. This explains why people who enter the ecstatic state complain that words cannot explain their experience. What cannot be said is part of the language of death.

For Sufism reveals also, through its relationship with language, its relationship with death.

Ecstasy takes its magic powers from death. For it represents – compressed into several moments – a sense of complete freedom from everything that separates the person in ecstasy from the Absolute, for whom he is searching and whom he is facing. This is what the Orpheus is referring to when he says that God lives in man, and that the death of the body is by itself capable of freeing him. 'After your death, you become God.' Ecstasy is nothing but the death of the body, but it is a temporary death.

Sexual frenzy is thus ecstasy; it is a transitory form of death or rather it is an image of death, its meaning. This is the most profound way in which two people are united. Each one emerges from himself and melts into the other. Sexual frenzy is, therefore, a second life, or a life inside life, or it is a superior form of real absent life. This frenzy is not only sensual, as it appears from the outside, but it is replete with things that go beyond feeling. Love through such delirium is as eternal as divinity or it is a part of it.

4

The Surrealists believe that love has an abundant means of transcending the three modes of existence (madness, dream, writing) and that, through love, man will come to know his true self, free himself from all restraints and raise himself up. The Surrealist view of love is founded on the principle of allowing free rein to desire and is inspired by three thinkers: Sade, who claimed to liberate desire, Freud, who formalized the instruments of critical liberation, and Marx, the theoretician of social liberty (Bartoli-Anglard, *Le Surréalisme*, p. 66).

The Surrealists believe that love is above all a dynamic principle; it frees up fantasies and takes away any feelings of guilt linked to the expression of desire. In eroticism the individual unveils his fantasies and discovers himself, through passionate upheaval (ibid. p. 67). But eroticism is not only based on passion and desire. Love is also the means of attaining the ideal and going beyond temporal limitations. It is the revelation of the self. The temptress, the *femme fatale* or the girl/woman is the one who will open the way to a live and concrete world. Love brings us to the essence, to the profound nature of being, which is revealed in our relationship to the other (ibid. p. 68). It is revolutionary in the sense that it breaks taboos and chains imposed by a society founded on false values.

Surrealist eroticism grew out of a desire to rebel against the formal law, imposed by the Christian ethic. Here we find the abandonment particular to Surrealism of what it calls contradictions: 'Finding the place and the formula' is 'to possess the truth in a soul and a body,' Breton says. Aragon says, 'There is a principle in love, which lies beyond the law ... a contempt for the disallowed and a taste for sacrilege' (quoted Bartoli-Anglard, ibid. p. 67). Love is the only value that allows man to encounter himself and meet a lost paradise, the paradise of unity, in which is reconstructed the being of a mythic androgyny (ibid., p. 67).

The Surrealists venerate woman and regard her as the chosen created being. She is fey and has a place in human mysticism, in which she appears as the great initiator. Women open the doors of paradise to poets, in which can be found forms and the essences in existence. Eroticism, as far as they are concerned, is not only an ethic but is also a philosophy, which rejects morals in order to bring about a revolution in the vision of men. Physical union is natural. It is necessary to rediscover this unity, which has been lost since the Fall (ibid., p. 69).

Woman is the one who allows fragmented man to become one with himself again. Love is an elevation towards the sacred. The idea of sanctity, Benjamin Peret says, flows so directly from love that, without it, sanctity is inconceivable (ibid., p. 70).

Passion permits man to rise above himself and it is woman who saves man from the banality of daily life because she embodies the mystery of her participation in cosmic life. She realizes the ambition of Surrealism to attain a non-objective man as if he had not been created. She also embodies complete freedom (ibid., p. 71).

Woman is therefore the future of man, his safety and his destiny (ibid., p. 72).

5

In Surrealism and Sufism, 'the one-the human' takes the place of 'the one-the absolute'. Thus the absolute is no longer the sole subject of love, but the beloved is the woman. The beloved's body is equivalent to the divine words. God in Sufism is a constant mystery; at that moment he is a constant presence. 'The beloved-the woman' is a mystery in the Surrealist experience. The language of love in Surrealism is the language of mystery. The woman is what cannot be obtained. She is secret or magical. The relationship of the lover to God is transformed into the relationship between lover and beloved. Love becomes a revelation, like the revelation that is realized through the divine words. The truth can be reached through the body of the beloved, as the truth can be reached through divine words. 'The beloved–the woman' is, like God, a mystery, an invisible being, who, in spite of being near, remains far off and eludes capture the moment someone is about to grab hold of her. The Sufi is fascinated by what he has not obtained and by what he has not realized. This is not because he is against what he has realized but because what he has realized is only a shadow or an image of a meaning that has not been enjoyed to the full and cannot be contained. He cannot realize what he wants. It continues to be a mystery. Subsequently death is absent from the image and present in the meaning, the faculty, by which he realizes what cannot be realized. In this sense, death is a second life; rather, it is a life that has no death after it.

What role does time play in all this? Time is the moment of revelation and change, the moment at which the Sufi is taken by the other – the beloved. It is the moment of intoxication, of nothingness. Therefore, the Sufi has defined time accordingly: 'Time is what you are in it.' It is different from chronological time, in any case.

Following on this, and within this context, it is possible to describe 'objective chance' as a collection of circumstances, which represent the extraordinary presences in daily life. It is the visible signs and warnings that prophesy the fusion of being and the oneness between man and being. In this sense it resembles Sufi revelation, by which I mean the moment when the divine presence is in existence, the moment during which the absent is made visible.

In such instances, reality and imagination melt into absolute reality, sur-reality, and dream and wakefulness meet in a particular elevated state. Such instances are very often associated with love. Love here has a much broader sense than sexual desire. It is the first emancipator of man and the first renewer of the world. As Breton asserts, there is no solution apart from love. The woman is the cornerstone of the material world and man's intermediary to the extraordinary world. Her love permits man to experience the attaining of the extraordinary. Because of that she is the earth – the mother. Breton says, 'We love the earth only through woman, and the earth in turn loves us. It recalls another saying of Ibn 'Arabi's: 'Every place that is not feminine cannot be trusted.'

# Writing

He pointed at me ... it was in his nature
not to speak to anyone except through symbols.
*Ibn 'Arabi*

If you don't stand behind the description,
the description will take you away.
*al-Niffari*

The more you see, the narrower the means of expressing it.
*al-Niffari*

## Ecstatic Pronouncement (*al-Shath*)

1

Sufism has laid the foundations for a form of writing that is based
upon subjective experience, in a culture that is generally based on
established religious knowledge. However, it has remained on the
margins of Arab cultural history. It has no particular location, as if
those who write it live not so much in a place as in their texts. The
text is the Sufis' homeland and their reality; it is as if they move

about inside this text and create in it and through it the world of which they dream.

The words are its secret paths, horizons and symbols. Through them, they turn towards the absent one and begin to talk with him – but through experience. They are not accustomed to using written words, instead of physical means, to talk to the Absolute. The discourse becomes a straight dialogue between the I and the you, between God and man. In this way the I begins to listen to the you, and enters a particular discussion with it, and looks up to and witnesses it, face to face, without the intermediaries of learning or tradition. This discussion itself is no more than a state. As such, it cannot be established. It is a state that is changing, not so much from one individual to another, because every individual has his own set of circumstances, but inside the individual, from one instant to another. Knowledge itself is a state. It has no permanence, i.e. it has no end. It rejects anything that is pre-set and narrow. The more we know of it, the less we feel we know. Whenever we are confident that we are drawing close to it, our bewilderment increases.

Thus Sufi gnosis/knowledge wells up out of the present, the here and now, and does not come from some past knowledge, which has been learned in the past and set down, but which is no longer able to respond to the present, for it is general knowledge, and what the present requires is knowledge derived from the uniqueness of experience and the distinctive period of time. This period of time is your time, that is, it is the time that contains you in it – you as a distinctive individual, in a distinct, historical moment. In the Sufi experience time is what lies between the past and the future and which contains you in it – it is 'the sword' or what 'annihilates you'.

Sufi writing, like Sufi knowledge, is no more than a history of a time, a history of the relationship between the I and the you or the history of the dialogue between the two. It is a knowledge that cannot be communicated, because it is irrational and derived from experience/taste. And as everyone has his own 'taste', so everyone has his own 'knowledge'. It is a certain kind of knowledge, which provokes the other to acquire his knowledge as well. It is not sufficient for the other to 'read' in order to know; instead he must 'live' and 'explore'. Knowledge is something to be uncovered and examined, not transferred. It is the present, not the past, and the now, not the day before, the here, not the there, the essence, not the whole and not the established.

2

Abu Nasser al-Sarraj defines *shath* (speaking in ecstasy) as 'a marvellous expression for describing ecstatic love, which boils up and overflows with the force of passion, and supremacy' (*Kitab al-Luma'*, Leiden, Nicholson, 1914, p. 346).

The word is not found in the *Lisan al-Arab* dictionary, for it comes from a post-classical age. It is commonly used to mean setting oneself apart, abandoning oneself to and departing from custom. Its original root is unknown.

Abd al-Rahman Badawi lists five necessary components for the existence of *shath*: 1. It must have the power of ecstatic ardour. 2. The experience must be the experience of oneness. 3. The Sufi must be in a state of intoxication. 4. He must hear within himself a divine voice calling him to oneness. 5. All of this must take place while the Sufi is unconscious, for he gives voice to and translates what appears to him and assumes the form of speaker, as if God were speaking through his mouth (Abd al-Rahman Badawi, *Shatahat al-Sufia*, Cairo, Maktabat al-Nahdah-al Misriyah, 1949, p. 4).

Al-Sarraj describes *shath* as follows: 'On the outside it appears dreadful but on the inside it is true and straight' (*al-Luma'*, p. 375). Al-Sarraj links the meaning of *shath* to movement. He says, '*shath* in the language of the Arabs denotes movement, for *shatahalyashtuhu* means 'he moved'/'he moves'. So *shath* is a word derived from movement, because it means the movement of the secrets of lovers when their passion becomes too powerful for them. They express their passions in phrases that astonish the person who hears them' (ibid., p. 308).

But there is a still form of ecstatic ardour that some Sufis prefer to movement. In his book on al-Wajd, Abu Sayyid bin al-'Arabi says that there are some kinds of ecstatic ardour 'which require stillness, and stillness here is better than movement. But some kinds of ecstatic ardour require movement, and movement is more perfect here since it overcomes those people who are in ecstasy. If they are not overcome, their inspiration will be weak as a result, for if it is a true emanation, it will require movement' (ibid.).

And he continues deliberating on which of the two is the better, saying, 'those who honour people who remain still are only honouring them because of their reason and the strength of their ability, and those who honour people who move prefer them because of the strength of the inspiration that is hidden from the understanding of reason, and the latter is more preferable owing to the inspiration. If two reasons are equal and neither one is better than the other, then, in that case, stillness is better than movement. However, I do not think that it is possible for two people to be the same, nor two reasons, nor two inspirations. Knowledgeable people reject such a situation. If such comparisons are void, then we are brought back to what we said previously when we started discussing this subject, and that is that it is meaningless to prefer stillness to movement or movement to stillness, because the state of inspiration that requires movement and the state that requires stillness are different. The state of the person does not depend on movement or stillness. If the state requires stillness and the person in that state doesn't become still, then he will not be as complete as the others. Or if the state requires movement and he doesn't move, then it indicates that he will lack inspiration' (ibid., p. 309).

3

*Shath* comes about as a result of ecstatic ardour and is stronger or weaker depending on how strong or weak the ecstatic ardour is; we should therefore look at the essence of ecstasy and its causes. Abd Allah al-Ansari of Harawi describes ecstasy as 'a fire that burns at the sight of something disturbing and there are three stages:

The first stage is a sudden attack of ecstatic ardour, which wakens the person who sees, hears or thinks it. It may or may not leave an impression on the person.

The second stage is an ecstatic ardour that wakens the soul with a flash of finite light or the sound of a primeval call or the sense of true attraction. It will either leave behind its cover for the person or leave behind its light.

The third stage is an ecstatic ardour that sweeps the slave (of God) out of the hand of the two universes and extracts its meaning from the dirt of luck. It saves him from the bondage of water and mud. If it saves him, it makes him forget his name. If it doesn't save him, it leaves its mark on him (*Kitab Manazil as-Sa'irin*, ed. Father Serge de Laugier de Beaurecueil, Cairo, Dominican Institute for Oriental Studies, 1962, pp. 76–77).

Ecstasy according to al-Ansari is the sixth stage of the ten stages of the states (*al-ahwal*): love, jealousy, desire, commotion, thirst, ecstasy, astonishment, mad love, illumination and taste (ibid., p. 71).

Zia Uddine al-Kamashkhanli defines ecstatic ardour as 'the burning flame of the fire of thirst, which wakens the soul with a flash of infinite light and exalted sight', in an almost exact repetition of what Ansari says (*Jami' al-Usul*, Cairo, 1920, p. 357).

As for the causes of *wajd*, they are many and varied. Abu Saied bin al-'Arabi says, '*wajd* (strong emotion) happens at the mention of something annoying, or when you are shaken by fear or being rebuked for a mistake or talking about something nice or indicating something useful, or longing for something missing, or sorrowing for something past or regretting something that is gone or recalling a state, or calling for a duty, or a secret conversation -confronting the manifest with the manifest and the concealed with the concealed, the mystery with the mystery, the secret with the secret, extracting what is yours and what you owe, what you have strived for in the past, and what is ordained for you because it is yours, as timelessness without timelessness and memory without memory are determined for you' (*al-Luma'*, p. 310).

If the aim of ecstasy is to establish 'memory without memory, timelessness without timelessness' for the person in ecstasy,[2] it means that his humanity will diminish to the point when nothing will remain of it except his divinity, and thus he, who is new, will become old and a memory, which will merge with the person who remembers and is remembered always, who is God. In other words, his 'absence' will unite with the 'absence' of God and they will become one. This explains why the path to oneness is full of suffering and pain, and why ecstasy itself is like a fire, burning the insides of the person who walks upon it. For it is a very long way, and each time he imagines that he has reached his destiny he realizes that the opposite is true, and that it is still a long way off. This increases the violence of his agitation and the ferocity of his disturbance and turmoil, the intensity of his movements and the longing to arrive, but without stopping and without despair. Togetherness here is unity. The humanity of man dissolves into it to remain in God as if he is divine.

4

Intoxication, as we pointed out, is a fundamental element in bringing about *shath*. Al-Ansari defines it as 'a word that is used to indicate the diminishing of self-control, when transported by delight. It particularly applies to the stages lovers pass through. The specifics of annihilation do not apply to it and the states of knowledge do not reach it.' 'There are three signs of intoxication,' he continues. 'He is distressed at what is happening, although he is more than capable of [bearing] it. He plunges into the surging sea of desire, although he can hold back. He drowns in a sea of happiness, although he has the patience to wait.

Anything apart from this is a form of bafflement, which has been given the name of intoxication in ignorance, or it is a sort of mad love, which is wrongly called intoxication. However, all such states are irrational, such as the intoxication of greed or the intoxication of ignorance or the intoxication of desire' (*Kitab Manazil al-Sa'irin*, ed. Beaurecueil, 1962, pp. 97–98).

Intoxication therefore simultaneously produces a state of mental and physical unconsciousness. It is a form of spiritual intoxication, and what results from it does not come about because the person is absent from his body but rather because of the effect of the spiritual presence, which makes absent, through the power of its illumination, the presence of the body. So it is not delirium, as people who accuse the Sufis and discredit *shath* claim, nor is it a devilish whispering or a confused murmuring, etc. It is the opposite of these. It is the state of openness between the Sufi and God, in which God discloses his secrets to the soul: God is the soul – the soul is God.

This unveiling is brought about, as Abd Rahman Badawi says, 'in the guise of some migrant wanderer or invisible caller who permits' the spirit to take the place of the other, 'so that it speaks through his tongue and announces that he exchanges love with love, and the I vanishes between them, so that both of them become one' (*al-Shatahat*, p. 11). And he criticizes Ibn Taymiyya, saying, 'it is wicked of him to delude us by comparing physical intoxication to spiritual intoxication [ibid.], in order to belittle the importance of the latter and discredit it.' Badawi criticizes Ibn Taymiyya, saying, 'some Sufis might pass through the state of minor extinction, intoxication and absence from the others. Intoxication is a state of love, which doesn't discriminate. He might say, in such a state, "Glory be to me", or "This *jubbah* (garment worn by dervishes) contains nothing except God", or other expressions like these, which have been reported as coming from Abu Yazid al-Bastami and other sober members of the

Sufis. Words spoken in the state of intoxication are hidden and are neither told nor counted' (*Majmu'at al-Rasa'il wal Masa'il*, vol. 1, p. 168). Badawi points out that the interchange of roles between slave and truth (Man and God) and the authorization of direct speech between them is a truly distinctive element in Islamic Sufism (*al-Shatahat*, p. 11) as compared to Christian and Jewish mysticism. Oneness is achieved through the interchange of roles: the essence of man dissolves into the essence of God, and ' his secrets will become uncovered and all the ill things in his heart will be expunged' (ibid., p. 13), and the existence of one of them will become the existence of the other, so that both of them will share the same name and the same attributes. There is no *shath* without this unity between Sufi and God.

Of course, there are those who deny that such a unity exists, since they deny the oneness of existence, and they say that God, whom the Sufi witnesses in this state of unity, in fact overpowers the Sufi, who witnesses him and extinguishes him with his light.

But the Sufis reply that such claims are similar to those made by people who deny the inner world as a whole or who have been unable to reach the state of *fana'*.[3]

Extinction in this oneness is the extinction of the I-ness, which means that the permanence of the I-ness is the permanence of what is seen (God), so that the Sufi sees himself in another form, 'and finds his essence like a pure feeling, which courses through the whole and is contained by the whole and finds it is the core of the whole' (Muhammad al-Amali, Baha'uddin bin Hussein bin Abd as-Samad, died 1621, *Majmu'at al-Rasa'il*, Cairo, Mohiddin al-Kurdi, pp. 320–21). At this stage, the Sufi reaches the state of knower, as Badawi points out (*al-Shatahat*, p. 14), for knowledge is the witnessing of truth (God) where the witness appears in front of God, but is unable to perceive him with his senses as they are absent (al-Kalabadhi, *al-Ta'arruf li Madhab Ahl al-Tasawwuf*, p. 104). Thus knowledge at its climax is nothing but *shath* and expressed through *shath*. Those who utter *shath* are regarded as the only people who possess knowledge.

Badawi says that the states, 'which run parallel with *shath* or pave the way to it', happen when the person is in an unconscious state. Consciousness here means being able to think logically. The states of Sufism do not actually depend on proof but on seeing and taste, and occur when a person is not conscious; this applies particularly to the psychic states connected with the phenomenon of *shath*, as being in a state of intoxication is the principal nerve that connects all these states, and intoxication is a state that happens when a person is unconscious. Thus, unconsciousness is a major element in defining the states necessary for *shath* (*al-Shatahat*, p. 14).

Although it lies outside our subject, we should point out that understanding *shath* poses many difficulties for those who read, criticize and interpret it. It is sufficient to point to a quotation, which demonstrates the difficulties faced by those who read *shath*. The text describes Abu Yazid al-Bastami who was the first person to establish *shath* writing. It says, 'The minds of people were impotent when it came to understanding his words, and individuals and people were bewildered when it came to understanding the meaning of his words. His words were uttered but no one understood what he meant, people described his marvels but his singularity was unknown, his details were collected but his facts went unheard, his expressions were understood, but his gestures were incomprehensible' (al-Sahlaji, in *Shatahat al Sufiya*, p. 46).

## Automatic Writing

## 5

How does the Surrealist attain the state of *shath* or the state that corresponds to it in Surrealist terminology? In trying to answer this question, I have referred to one book on Surrealism in particular, so

I shall leave it to the author of this book to respond to the question, and it will be sufficient as far as I am concerned to present what she says and some extracts from her book (Bartoli-Anglard, *Le Surréalisme*).

The writer says that the revolution, as far as Surrealism is concerned, originates with language in which a new aesthetic is born, derived from creative practice (ibid., p. 43). Thus, it is necessary 'to restore language to its true life,' as Breton says. Therefore they have to 'explore the mechanics of spontaneous creation and resort to automatism [involuntary writing], under the dictates of the unconscious'. To put it another way, they have to 'begin with a way of writing that is opposed to literary practices and from there define a new aesthetic, in order to restore to words the paradise that has been lost' (ibid.).

The Surrealists follow three methods to achieve this spontaneous creativity: dream narration, hypnotic sleep and automatic writing, i.e. writing carried out without the control of the will (ibid.). Hypnotic sleep at first appeared to be the most authentic way of arriving at this psychic automatism, as (with dream narration) man had to remember the dream in order to write it down, but not only did the act of remembering require a sort of willpower, but also memory could twist the dream.

Automatic writing (unconscious writing) was at first regarded as being similar to the dream state but rapidly became the 'preferred tool of research'. It was not possible to be a Surrealist poet without practising automatic writing.

In 1924, Breton writes in the *First Surrealist Manifesto* that automatic writing is an excellent means of producing a poetic text by exercising 'pure psychic automatism'. Automatism is in fact a superior technique to dream narration. 'It allows the person to reproduce the discourse that is constantly running in our unconscious and of which we are not aware.' In order to understand ourselves better, we must free ourselves from social censure and moral censure' (ibid., p. 44). Breton believes that thought can be expressed as quickly in writing as in speech. To speed up the creative process, the writer has to obtain a 'verbal outpouring', which is precipitated by internal residue (Breton, *First Surrealist Manifesto*).

Automatism therefore not only contributes to speed but also frees up thought. It demands that we write without obeying any moral or aesthetic rule. It allows us to regain the lost powers of imagination and better to understand how the mechanisms of thought are developed. Automatic writing turned out to be the most fertile means of exploring the unconscious. It is therefore both a means of writing and a way of better understanding oneself (Bartoli-Anglard, p. 44).

The Surrealists believe that reflecting on language is an instrument in the struggle for freedom and for authentic expression. Therefore they do not look at it as 'a means of communication' or 'an element of social alienation' but rather as 'a tool for self-discovery' (ibid., p. 45).

The collective character of certain of those works inspired by the practice of automatic writing bears witness as well to the democratic character of the artistic function. Thus, as Valery and Borges say, 'literary work does not have a single author but is the result of or production by a universal thought. Each author embraces the culture that has gone before him and directs it to produce his text, which will in turn be enriched by the personal reading of each reader of it.' 'Poetry will be the deed of everyone,' as Lautréamont says (ibid., p. 45).

If automatic writing permits one to explore the imagination, on the one hand, and to reflect on the psychic processes, on the other (ibid., p. 47), then it is clear that the linguistic signs that are fixed through custom demand social criticism, and it is also clear that the signs produced by the practice of automatism take on a meaning which needs to be analysed (ibid., p. 48). The Surrealists wish to exercise their critical faculties and refuse to be satisfied with exercising reason or non-reason alone (ibid.). This means they rejected the moral codes in order to practise a reasoned disorder of psychic automatism, so as to arrive at a new clarity. Automatism should provide every individual with the means of arriving at an internal truth and, at the same time, understanding his true nature in relation to his human nature. As Lautréamont puts it, 'Automatism returns the sense of the whole to the individual.' It makes him speak a lost language, that of unconscious desire, which however is common to all men (ibid.).

Therefore automatism is 'an exercise, which enables the writer to suppress the screens of reason and to attain the lost powers of psychic life.' It permits him to clarify the rapport that links the id (me) to the unconscious (ibid.). According to Freud, man appears practically non-existent, torn apart as he is by dark forces on the one hand, and censured by social morality on the other. The Surrealists believe that, 'automatism rehabilitates the subject and enriches man by forcing him to struggle to capture it' (ibid.).

Aragon says, 'Man must strive to reach what lies beyond reality, though he will never realize it as it will always escape him.' Breton appears more optimistic, when he writes in the Manifesto, 'Man must use all his powers of reason and imagination and devote himself to it' (ibid.). In this way, the poet becomes a visionary and in his psychic life explores places that have no limitations. 'Automatic writing therefore has an active function; it renders possible the exploitation of all possibilities' (ibid., p. 49). Breton says in this context, 'For such writing to be truly automatic, the writer must in fact have succeeded in detaching himself from the demands of the outside world as well as individual mundane preoccupations such as order, sentiment, etc' (ibid.). Such a radical detachment is not simple. There is an additional difficulty: since language is the fixed instrument of official education, how can automatic production, which is also linguistic, ensure the existence of a human language in the pure form that the Surrealists gave themselves the task of recovering? This is particularly true, as Breton says, 'since all we know is that we have been gifted to a certain degree with language, and that something big and obscure is persistently trying to make itself known by words about itself, through us' (ibid.).

The Surrealists do not forget to point to the dangers that automatic writing might present: the individual, who watches himself as he writes, will become in turn a spectator of himself, and the visionary poet might be tempted to transform himself into a prophet (ibid., p. 50).

The Surrealists are not satisfied with reaching what lies behind the material world through writing but work on practising the art of poetry, which will make visual what lies beneath. Maurice Blanchot says, 'Automatic writing [mechanical writing] is only a means for making real this golden age, which Hegel called absolute bliss, the passing from the night of possibility to the day of presence' (ibid., p. 51).

Although the Surrealists work to change the vision into things, they do not change anything in the structure of the language. In fact, on the contrary, they renew it and give it a new means of expression. Aragon and Eluard, however, realize that automatism is not sufficient on its own, but that it is necessary to adopt a conscious poetic art, which can be practised in a controlled way and to reform what automatic writing gives. Aragon says, 'I demand that the dreams that are presented to me to read should be written in good French' (ibid.).

6

Imagination in the Surrealist sense of the word is what allows one to attain the sur-real (what is behind reality). The imagination of surrealism, according to Julien Gracq, is nothing to do with reverie and waking dreams. 'It is a major power, sovereign and uncontrollable, a decisive protest against reality, a supreme authority through which the opaque insignificance of the external world is cited and condemned' (ibid.). This faculty, which imagination represents, makes it possible to realize fantasies by giving them form. The dream allows the sleeper to evolve according to his desires. The madman lives constantly in a dream state. Love opens up the gates of the sur-real in the world. Surrealism is a cultural revolution, which breaks the chains of thought. At issue here is, as Aragon says, 'a new declaration of the rights of man', whereby he will agree to modify his behaviour in order to bring about a reconciliation between imagination and real life and resolve the contradictions between them, so as to overcome them and attain the sur-real (ibid.).

This revolution also changes the function of poets. 'The poet is the one who inspires rather than the one who is inspired,' says Paul Eluard. In this way the Surrealists link the enfranchisement of man to a new form of education, founded on a fertile approach, which teaches man to be himself, to know himself and to work to realize that in a conscious fashion. Among the tasks of the poet is to make it possible for others to attain this lost paradise that is sur-realism. In fact, the rejection of reality poses an essential question. 'What is it that makes life worth living?' The answer lies in the power of the living spirit, the dreams, the faculty of desire and love; together, they open the way to a superior dimension. For surrealism is 'the encounter between the temporal aspect of the world and its eternal values – love, freedom and poetry' (ibid., p. 58). The Surrealists go on to search for a new form of the world, in a new vision. It is a matter of modifying the conditions of perceiving reality, adopting another approach to things in disorder, as happens in the fantastic and in madness, and extracting from love a new energy, which will transfigure the world in its entirety (ibid.).

Aragon says in his *Treatise on Style*, 'We write in order to speak to ourselves and to know ourselves, and in order to exist. It is not a question of making a poem a simple transcription of a dream, but of forging a new way of writing' (ibid.). A new logic is born out of the intricacies of dreams and reality. It is necessary to avoid the abstract, which distances us from life, and to search instead in the surprising proximity among the images for a means of rediscovering authenticity.

Poetic images are nothing more than forms of linkage between the visible and the invisible (ibid.). The unconscious originally dictates the image. Surprise is one of the fundamental tenets of the surrealist aesthetic. It is the encounter with the unknown, with the riches of the world and of beings. Apollinaire saw that surprise represented the dynamic of the new thought (ibid., p. 59).

The image makes possible the concrete translation of reality. It allows one to go beyond the power of reason and it gives form to an individual perception of the world. It brings together two ways of perceiving the world, without elevating one over the other. According to Breton, it opens up the way to all possibilities, through illogical powers (ibid.). The Surrealists lay great faith in language and its powers. Language structures our vision of the world and our relationship to words opens up new horizons in front of us. Thus 'language is transformed into a revelation (prophecy) and leads us into the Babel of our thoughts,' as Breton says (ibid., p. 61).

7

Is automatic writing (I shall stick here to the commonly used phrase, pointing out that I prefer the term 'unconscious writing') in this context an attempt to find an answer to the question: 'What is the supreme point?', which is a question whose definition preoccupied Breton, or is it, on the contrary, nothing more than the starting point to this question?

In any case, the Surrealists, like the Sufis, affirm that literature as far as they are concerned contains a profound meaning only if one goes beyond the literal form into the mysteries of the universe. The essence of literature lies in its magical, transformative dimension, which aims at transforming man into an enlightened being. The role of literature is not to create texts that are pleasant and beautiful in themselves but to create with and through them a magical and enchanted process and bring about a transformation, so as to establish an enlightened linkage between, on the one hand, the depths of the unknown in man and, on the other, the universe.

The Surrealists, like the Sufis, therefore see their task as one of revelation rather than beautification. This is because this revelation is itself beauty.

This enables us to understand the importance of automatic writing; it is not just an overflowing of the unconscious, but a message, the supreme device through which objective chance, which is the mystery of the universe or the spirit of the world, is revealed to man.

It is not possible therefore to assess automatic writing (like *shath*) without linking it to objective chance. Language in automatic writing (speech) is not just language, but it is an extension of the word or a universal language (*shath* is a universal language in that the universe speaks through it, through its Sufi speaker) and poetry here is not speech, but rather it is a magical, transformative work (deed), whose goal is to share in the original mystery of creation. In order to achieve this, Surrealism, like Sufism, ordains that man should cut himself off from the mundane world and mundane consciousness, in order to be able to go far beyond the unknown.

Nothing has any value except this disappearance into an inner jewel, which is neither the soul of ice nor the soul of fire (Breton), and this disappearance is the same as Sufi ecstasy. The jewel is itself the 'supreme point' in which distinctions between opposing forces, between fire and stone and animal disappear, and at which man becomes a being of light, a divinely illuminated point.

Thus we see that automatic writing is not merely a linguistic question but that it also reveals many things that are linked to the self, and the places in which unbounded desire surges up. This form of writing, as Eluard says, continuously opens up new doors on to the unconscious and brings it face to face with the conscious and the world, and adds to its richness. It is able at the same time to renew this conscious and this world.

Among the Surrealists, automatic writing continued to be the principal method of exploring the unconscious, but nevertheless it did not achieve what Breton expected of it.

Automatic writing is spontaneous, unstudied, free from any form of the compulsion that arises from a censuring mind, critical thought and analogous words. Automatic writing is freedom from the mundane and its obstacles. It pushes the writer to leave his familiar self for another space.

Maurice Blanchot says, 'Automatic writing was intended to suppress restraint and repel any intervention or intermediaries, to place the hand that writes in contact with something original, to make out of this active hand a sovereign passivity, not a 'pen-hand' – an instrument, an obedient tool, but an independent force, over which no one has any control and which belongs to no one, and which no longer has the power to do or know anything – except write. It is a dead hand, which resembles the hand of triumph, which magic talks about ...

'That is what automatic writing means to us in particular: the language that enables us to become close to it is not power, not the power of speech. It is not the language I speak. I don't speak in it at all. One of the characteristics of normal speech is that hearing is part of its nature. But at this point of the experience, hearing does not play a role in language. In this lies the risk of the poetic function. The poet is someone who listens to the language without hearing it' (Béhar and Carassou, *Surréalisme: Textes et Discussions*, Paris, Librairie Générale, 1984, p. 183).

Thus it appears that what the Surrealists understand by automatism is contradictory to its apparent sense, for it is a form of non-concentration, an absence of thought, or a vacuity, in which the conscious dissolves, and whose role is limited to receiving what comes to it: it receives what is sent to it by the unconscious, the unaware, and records it.

In this case, strictly speaking, automatism can be compared to the Sufi state of *shath*; it is a state that comes in the absence of reason, in the state of ecstasy and intoxication.

But if consciousness does not play an active role in a state such as this, among some Sufis, it does continue to play a role when the person is awake and alert, when it opens up a way that joins him to the unconscious and enables him to receive the fruit of the dream – the produce of the world, which has escaped rational conscious censorship. Consciousness here is a tool for exploring what is behind it: the unconscious, the abstract, the invisible – in man and in things – because his unconscious is linked to the unconscious of things. The unconscious here and the conscious are one with no separation between them. This oneness is alien to Western thought. Perhaps we might find it in Malcolm de Chazal and a few like him, but it is derived from Sufi ideas, not from Western culture. The discovery of the invisible in the visible itself, of the unconscious in the conscious, of the meaning in the image: this is the ideative force – the gnosis – which is peculiar to Sufism. The conscious-the unconscious, the visible-the invisible, the image-the meaning: interconnected, inseparable.

But in order to be able to attain this state, it is necessary for thought to attain a high peak from which it will descend to the other side, to the invisible, so as to see the invisible side of things. Not only does the object reflect the man, but man also reflects the object: the object sees the man, just as man sees the object. Man becomes an image, he sees himself in objects and the whole world is revealed to him.

Like *shath,* at first appearance, automatic writing negates the classical tradition of writing and collides with those minds that have been brought up on such writing. It does not only clash with literary reasoning but also with habitual reasoning, or what is meant usually by 'common sense'. Automatic writing differs from rational writing in several ways.

1. It is not preceded by thought, in other words, there is no prior writing or design.

2. It is not controlled by the conscious mind or reason.

3. It does not follow a traditional written order: the writing appears, externally, to be chaotic, without any order or content.

4. It does not subscribe to aesthetic or moral concerns (in the classical sense of the word).

5. It is a flood of words. Such writing is like an outpouring of being, an outpouring of the unconscious, ungoverned by any restraints. Breton refers to it as 'the enchanted hopes'

(*Les pas perdus*, see Béhar and Carassou, p. 190) and it can be compared to what the Sufis describe as 'dictation'. It is not surprising that these 'hopes' or 'dictating' or '*shath*' have been described as words that have no sense of beauty and that are scattered about in disarray, superficially expressing some morsels of memory, scraps of ideas and peculiar fantasies and which are against religion and ethics.

In this context, the Surrealists affirm the primacy of language not only as a means of communication but also as a means of expression and working. The Surrealists say that if language had not betrayed us, we would be able to speak completely, without barriers, and know ourselves for what we are, beyond social conventions. When this knowledge is re-established, people will understand each other, directly and clearly, and it will be possible to transform the world in communion with each other.

For the Surrealists believe that language is a form of 'original language', as Rousseau claims. The world and the things of the universe are created by the divine word – although Surrealism eliminates any concept of origin that lies outside man. Language disappears as a tool because it has become the essence itself; it is mingled with thought. The freedom of man himself has become dynamic, revealed. It is not possible to regard language as something functional. Explaining the opinion of the Surrealists, Blanchot says, 'We cannot use it for expression. Because it is free and is freedom itself.' In this way, the word and freedom become a unity that cannot be divided, and language takes on a special life; it attains a hidden power, which is able to escape man's understanding.

The Surrealist belief that language is an underground river, which they have a duty to bring to light, led them to approach the issue of inspiration in terms that were different from those employed by the Romantics. As they see it, the river belonged to everyone and it was sufficient for man to know how to listen to its murmur.

8

I hope I have gone some way to explaining the position of writing in the Surrealist experience. Like Sufi writing, it appears for the most part to be filled with strange things, contradictions, obscure references and disjointed images that are difficult to understand. So disjointed are some of them that some people have accused the Surrealists of picking them arbitrarily and confusing them.

But such critics forget that the anarchic, the astonishing, the baffling and the obscure form the basis for Sufi (and Surrealist) writing and such writing does not exist without such forms. This is not the result of an aesthetic or philosophical way of thinking, but it is an organic part of the writing itself, because this writing describes a world that is itself strange and bewildering and obscure. It is a form of writing, a labyrinth belonging to a world, that is itself a world – a labyrinth. When the poet enters a world of transformations, he can leave it only by transformative writing: waves of illuminating images, which do not bear scrutiny by reasonable or logical means, and through which reality itself is transformed into a dream.

# The Aesthetic Dimension

The glance perhaps addresses the onlooker with
what expression cannot convey, nor translation carry.

*al-Niffari*

1

If we start by saying that God is not known except by God, or by
saying that no one knows God except God, then man's knowledge
of God will constantly need to exceed itself and be renewed in order
to remain equal to what it is striving to comprehend, which is the
unlimited nature of God and his infinity. If God is a continuous
mystery, then knowing him must be a continuous revelation.

Therefore, he is a mystery, who continues to be a mystery.
He is self-existent and independent. It is impossible to place him
in a finite image, for he is larger than any knowledge. Language
cannot contain him; it can only convey an idea of him or convey
the experience of seeing and understanding him. Nevertheless, what

it conveys can be conveyed only in a circuitous fashion: through images and symbolism, allusions and references.

Man is not merely an object or a date; he contains in himself something that is greater than himself. His identity is hidden in this mystery. Man is a product of history, but inasmuch as he is a mystery, he transcends it.

This mystery is simultaneously an absolute presence. It is apparent, visible in revelations, which are but sparks of light that point towards it. It is different from what we call the unknown. The unknown can be known, but this mystery cannot be reached by knowledge, nor can it be entirely comprehended. We know only images of it, but its essence remains a mystery.

2

The absent/the present is the domain in which man's visual and visionary powers operate. It is the area of illumination on which the Sufi aesthetic is based.

This aesthetic is based on two principles:

1. Man's attempts to reveal the mystery only result in a greater need of it. What he knows is the merest fragment of what remains unknown, which demands to be known. The more he knows, the more ignorant he becomes, i.e. the more desperate to penetrate the mystery.

2. The experience of illumination must be expressed in words that are free from the constraints of reason and logic and shared common things, and free from sectarian theology and orthodox precepts. Illumination is something that cannot be spoken, something that cannot be described. It is from another state.

3

It should be added that the Sufi aesthetic sense rests on contradictions. This means that the object can only explain its essence by contradicting it. Death in life and life in death, day in night and night in day. The opposites meet in complete oneness: movement and stillness, reality and imagination, the strange and the familiar, the lucid and the obscure, the interior and the exterior.

The Sufi unites the interior and the exterior, the self and the object, hidden reality and enlightened reality, so in order to attain the state of exalted inspiration, this state will not be revealed to a specific individual but to every individual.

This oneness between the visible world and the invisible world is the oneness of two opposites, and it is one of the basic tenets of the aesthetic of Sufi writing.

Thus we see that in the Sufi aesthetic, there is something that compels man continuously to go forward, to go beyond the limits that restrain him, to go beyond the known. As he moves forward, he must constantly renew himself, so that he will remain an eternal presence, eternally ready to advance towards the unknown.

4

What method does Sufism use to achieve illumination?

In order to answer that, we must distinguish between knowledge that comes from reason/the intellect and knowledge that comes from the heart. The former is used to understand the external world, the world of phenomena, and the second to understand the inner, essential world. It follows, therefore, that we must distinguish between the world of religious law and the world of real meaning. Reason uses particular methods, such as analysis and proof, to acquire knowledge. The heart, for its part, uses intuition, illumination and taste.

Sufism rejects not only rational methodology but also the way of life based on its criteria, in order to be able to penetrate deeper into what cannot be defined and has no end.

Sufism confounds the external order of the world and its tools of knowledge, as it confounds the familiar order of words, in the way it expresses things. Sufism does not establish rational relationships between itself and nature and its things, but rather regards nature as a collection of symbols, images and references to which it relates through its heart – in the Sufi sense of the word.

The Sufi voices his sense of illumination or gives expression to it in a language that emerges as a flood, a dictation or *shath*, which is almost completely unchecked by reason. In spite of that, the writings of Sufism are not meaninglessness but are a wish for ecstatic illumination. This experience is at times revealed through expressions, words and images, which may be termed apostasy or trickery by people who look at them from the outside, or through the prism of orthodoxy. The experience crosses over from the partial to the whole, thereby transcending the dualism of matter and spirit, the apparent and the concealed and moving towards a oneness, in which illumination is joined with work and ecstasy with living practice.

Sufi writing does not present ideas in the abstract philosophical meaning of the word, but only presents states and moods; it does not compute or educate, but agitates things and explodes their mysteries.

Poetry according to this aesthetic is like a breeze, blowing across the world, in which creativity bursts forth and permeates the life in everything, and in which the barriers between the I and the other, the self and the object, cease to exist and the opposites are in harmony with each other.

5

In Sufi writing, the I and the non-I melt into one, in a dialectic movement, which transforms man himself into a movement that seeks out the hidden part of existence and merges with its secrets. This writing appears more distant than the literariness of speech. It appears to be a word that snatches at what lies behind nature, as if it is a secret atmosphere in what is behind the words. It appears to be waiting for something that is unexpected, to be wishing for something that will be not fulfilled, for when it realizes what it is yearning for, this only increases the sense of longing and urgent solicitation. When we immerse ourselves in such writing, we ask whether the language is audible or touching, whether it is really revelatory or profound. Everything in it appears to be a symbol, a dream or a sign. Night is not night so much as an allusion to another light, and death is not death so much as another life.

This is very apparent in the outpourings of *shath,* which flood out from the unknown world inside man, and which religious reason in particular has fought and written about. It is strange that this 'reason', which believes in djinn and invisible worlds and beings, does not also believe in the existence of a world in the human body that reason cannot see or encompass.

*Shath* sheds light on this great world, which is filled with what is sudden and dazzling, with what is infinite. It is an explosive force, which destroys the familiar patterns of thought and expression and writing. It is like a light, which pierces through logic and its analogies and enables man to get to know the internal invisible world of nature. However, orthodox religious reason believes that penetrating the mysteries of nature and the transcendental qualities of nature and man is a property of prophetic inspiration and is peculiar to it. They therefore ordain that writing must remain within the boundaries of the apparent known, so that it will not enter into competition with prophecy and risk refuting it.

This brings us to the premise that the aesthetic of Sufi writing is similar to the aesthetic of Surrealist writing, in that they both fundamentally rely on figurative language. This is because they are basically unorthodox forms of writing. The first contravenes religious orthodoxy while the second contravenes the established socio-cultural orthodoxy.

Since figurative language is ambiguous, it does not provide any conclusive answers. It is, in fact, a battleground on which the struggle over contradictory meanings is played out. Figurative language only raises more questions. From the point of view of knowledge, it is an element that is troubling and disturbing, rather than one that is serene and calm. This helps to explain why there is such opposition to figurative language in religious circles, in particular, in Arab culture. There is a viewpoint, which still holds sway, that either rejects interpretation, i.e. figurative language, and understands the religious text, literally, or it accepts figurative language but on condition that any answer that conflicts with the orthodox view is outlawed. In both cases, prime position is given to the text, which must be obeyed. Interpretation according to this viewpoint is only a confirmation of what conforms with the given, direct, literal meaning of the text. Interpretation here is a form of analytical work, which proves the text and what it contains, and does not raise questions about it or interpret it in such a way as to conflict with the literal and orthodox meaning.

The poetical nature of figurative language lies in the fact that it is not attributable to any source, i.e. it is innovative, as if it is constantly beginning and has no past. With its capacity to raise questions, it renews man in that it renews thought and language and relations to things. It is a movement that denies a present existence in its search for another existence. Figurative language transcends: just as the language it uses transcends itself, so too does the reality that it is explaining transcend itself. Thus figurative language links us to another dimension of things – its invisible dimension.

Figurative language naturally demands a dynamic of reading, which will complement its dynamism, since reading, like figurative language, is constantly innovative. Reading that merely insists on a literal or superficial understanding of the text contradicts the very nature of language, since literalism destroys a text, in image and meaning, as well as destroying man and his ideas. On this level, it is possible to say that the text is its interpretation. To put it another way, no interpretation or figurative language is intended to provide conclusive and solid facts such as can be found in religious, scientific and mathematical texts. Religious parties are the most hostile to figurative language, since they are interested in what they call the facts, which they preach and explain in their entirety. Figurative language is imaginary, which in their view means that it is wrong and meaningless.

However, figurative language from the point of view of the Sufis and the Surrealists is not just a stylistic form but also a vision. Arab writing describes figurative language as follows: a person will be fascinated by a phrase whose meaning is incomplete and which is represented figuratively, and he will long to complete it. However, if the person reads something whose meaning is instantly clear and which contains no figurative language, then he will no longer wish to know more (Bahrajani). For what is known generates a desire for what is not known. Figurative language generates a desire to obtain the whole or to go out from the finite to the infinite. Therefore, the structure of writing in Sufism and Surrealism rests on a language that prompts enquiry and questions, as well as a desire to know the unknown and enter into the movement of infinity. Thus the dimension of infinity in expression is an answer to the dimension of infinity in knowledge.

6

Talking about figurative language leads us on to image. Image has assumed a deep significance in the writings of both Sufis and Surrealists. It discloses God (meaning) or it is what raises the veil that exists between him and us so that we see him and become joined to him. This disclosure does not mean that meaning is any more revealed, or that it is transferred from the realm of the absent to the realm of the present, but rather that its appearance is modified, and it is more visible. The brighter and more brilliant the sun becomes, the less we are able to look at it; in other words, it is hidden from the eye. In this sense, we can understand the Sufi when he says, 'In the intensity of appearance lies concealment.' Image is like a fine, diaphanous mist, which veils meaning, so that it becomes possible to look at it and so that it 'manifests itself' to the seer.

But the appearance of meaning is concealed because its light is veiled when it appears in an image, since the image is a limited evocation of what is limitless. Meaning (God) is not absent; we say that it is present or it is apparent, because it is a constant absolute presence. When we see God in an image, we are not seeing him-as himself, we are seeing only our image in him. The image comes from the seer, not from what is seen. Meaning is veiled in the state of its appearance, and it is apparent in the state of its being veiled. However, it is veiled not by anything outside itself but by its own light. The veiling is the result of the strength of the appearance: the light is dazzling, to the extent that it is impossible for the eye to gaze or look at it.

Therefore, the image is a light that is condensed by the force of meaning (God) and his willingness to enable us to become acquainted with his essence, his qualities and his names. It makes known the meaning (God) because it is concealed by his great kindness, which cannot be understood or known. Since the image is a veil, it will refer us back to the light of meaning and the darkness of the universe simultaneously. Image and universe are clouds that cover the sun of meaning, but are, at the same time, a way towards it. It is the apparent that points to the inner. Therefore, those who are content to look at it, within the limits of the sensory apparent, do not see meaning as light, but darkness, while those who go beyond these limits and penetrate through to its inner meaning will see meaning in its true light and true existence.

Image, in this sense, rescues the perceptible universe, for it would diminish and be consumed by fire, if the light of meaning were to appear. When the fineness appears, the thickness disappears. This is what is meant by God's commandment to Moses. When Moses asked to see him, God told him to look at the mountain and see how it bore only a fraction of his divine light. People are able to look at meaning (God) in the perceptible world only through an image, that is, through sensory intensity. The image therefore is the domain of attributes and density. The essence is known through the attribute, and the fineness is known through the thickness.

7

Ibn 'Arabi sees that the spiritual world appears in images perceived by the senses. He says, for example, that, 'when a djinni[1] appears in a sensory image, eyesight will enchain it in such a manner that it will not be able to leave this image while the eye [of the man] is looking at it specifically, but through the man. When the eye enchains the spirit and continues to watch it, and the spirit has no place in which to disappear, the spirit shows the man an image, which it places over him like a curtain. Then it makes him imagine that this image is walking off in a particular direction, so the man's eyes follow it, and as his eyes follow it, the spirit leaves its shackles and disappears. As it disappears, the image vanishes from the gaze of the person who is looking at it and following it with his eyes. The image of the spirit is like the light of a lamp shining in a corner. If the body of the lamp is taken away, then the light vanishes as well; the same thing happens with the image. Who knows this, and wants to hold on to the spirit, will not allow his eyes to be diverted by an image. This is one of the divine secrets, which can be known only through a knowledge of God. The image is no more than the essence of the spirit; rather, it is the essence itself, even though it is in a thousand places, or everywhere, or in different forms. If it comes to pass that one of these images is killed and dies externally, the spirit is conveyed from the life of this world to the intermediate world, as we are conveyed in death, and there will be no further mention of it in the temporal world, as we have. These sensory images in which the spirits appear are called materializations.'

Perhaps we should regard the image as a shadow. In religious tradition, God is a shadow/umbra over the earth. This tradition is generally accepted: 'Authority is the shadow of God over the earth, when he appears with all the images of the divine names that have a trace in the temporal world. The throne is the shadow of God in the other world.'[2]

The shadow follows the image that originates from it, in sense and meaning. Sense is restrictive; it constrains and limits; therefore the semantic shadow of the abstract image is stronger and more expressive than it.

Beings also have shadows, which worship God.[3] In this sense they are those who populate the world. The concept of shadows can be explained by looking at what happens when Muhammad separates from his creator; when he separates from God, the place in which he is separated is inhabited by his shadow because there is no emptiness in this world.[4] As he separates from the light, he appears. When he faces the light by himself, his shadow extends and inhabits the space left by his separation. The shadow is an indication that he is still connected to his creator. Thus Muhammad is visible to the one towards whom he moved, on separating, which is man, and he witnesses him, from whom he separated, and that is the creator. Thus it is true to say that he exists in every place.

Perhaps we should regard the image as the outcome of a relationship between the thing that is affecting and the thing that is affected by it. The thing that is affecting holds the position of father and is the spirit, while the thing that is being affected holds the position of mother, and she also represents nature – the place of transformation. The father is supreme while the mother is of lower rank.

The image is what links the natural human union between father and mother to the union of spiritual composition between pen and preserved tablet (the place and location of writing), or between primordial reason and the soul in its entirety; if we consider the symbol of the writer (primordial reason) and the intention of the writing (the dispersal of knowledge – the marriage of natural union), we can understand what is meant by the words 'God created Adam in his image' and what is meant by what God, the most high, said when he created things: 'Be [k-n]'. The *kaf* (k) and the *nun* (n) are primordial reason and the soul in its entirety – two forewords, between which there is a concealed link, which binds them together as *k-n*, which Ibn 'Arabi describes as the omitted letter *waw* (u) because k and n are silent letters. What comes from *k-n* is exactly the outcome: the image. For there is a marriage of meaning between pen and tablet, which leads to the sensory effect, which are the letters. This helps us to understand what Imam al-Sadeq is talking about when he says that God created the letters first: the sensory trace, laid down on the tablet, is only the water of knowledge (=creation), and it is symbolized by the water gushing forth from the womb. Meaning inhabits the letters, as the spirits of children inhabit their bodies.

In the same way, when the father and mother (the man and the woman) meet, the pen disappears and the sperm is mysteriously tossed into the womb, because it is secret. The marriage is also secret. Whether it is in the world of nature or in the world of words, the image is the outcome of the relationship or the result. The speaker is the father and the listener is the mother, and the word is what ties them together (the marriage), and the son is what the listener understands: the new image or the result. In the world of natural human union, the father becomes the actor (the one who brings into being) and the mother, the woman, is the one who is acted upon, and marriage is the act of becoming, and the child is the result of this action.

Understanding images is nothing more than an extraordinary form of visual understanding. This explains the story that was told about how some pebbles Muhammad held in his hand invoked the Lord. God gave him and his companions who were present the power to listen to this prayer. The pebbles praised God since God created them, but the ability to hear the prayer was a form of abnormal auditory perception, which did not come from the pebbles (*al-Futuhat*, p. 155:1).

In Muhammad, there are two qualities – the quality of knowing and the quality of doing. Through the quality of doing, he gives images, which are of two kinds, sensory phenomena, like embodiments, forms and colours linked to them, and spiritual inner meaning, which is what it contains from knowing and knowledge and desires. And the quality of knowing is the domain of the father because it is affective and the quality of doing is the domain of the mother because it is what is affected. The image is the result of both qualities.

Thus image is a symbol of gnosis rather than identity or existence. With an image, man imagines the meaning embodied in himself, and this embodiment makes the transference of meaning easier, because of the force of its happening in the imagination. Ibn 'Arabi says that the embodiment of the image forces man to examine it until he understands the meaning as a whole. For once the meaning assumes image and form, the senses fall in love with it and gaze on it and amuse themselves with it and that will lead the person to realize what the form is aimed at and what the image represents for him (*Insha' al-Dawa'ir*, pp. 5–6).

8

Let us say that image is the bringing closer of what is far away, or rather it is the proximity that keeps the meaning distant. This proximity is apparent not only in the explanation, but also in the mystery and the distance. The infinite is generated by the integral confrontation between what is revealed and what is a mystery, between image and meaning, between proximity and distance. It is as if the thought always takes shape in the dividing line between meaning and image, which is like the dividing line between light and darkness. But man is always taken towards meaning or light. That is because seeing defines but does not create. Seeing therefore is no more than a threshold to what lies further away: the mystery. When he can see the most, man finds that his thirst for what he has not yet seen becomes more intense. Seeing is movement of infinite things: the point of arriving is the point at which we discover how far away it is, rather than how near, and how much we still thirst for it, rather than that our thirst is quenched. Nearness is a gleam of light in which distance appears to be further away, and the furthest point of nearness is death: death, which eliminates life in this world and sets up life in the other world. The other life is death with respect to the shadow – this world, but it is life with respect to the light – the other. Absence from shadow is only presence in light. So death is light: death is the existence of truth. The past is light, and the present is *barzakh* – the image, and the future is death – everlasting life. But the past here is not a point that has passed or ceased, rather it is the root or origin in front of man. The past in this sense is the future that has come, and the present is the future that is coming and the future is the future that will come. Time is this movement of shadow-light, which measures concealed-overt existence. Existence is no more than a continuous movement of the opposing forces of the concealed-overt, the overt-concealed (the apparent-hidden, the hidden-apparent).

Man himself is an intermediate state (*barzakh*), a bridge between shadow and light, and his existence lies at the centre of the crossing towards the light. His life is an everlasting impatience to cross. He appears to exist between two limits: he cannot live without the absence in front of him, which conceals his limitations, but paradoxically, he cannot move towards life without an image, which he sees and which reveals how to unite himself with the mystery.

The mystery transcends man but simultaneously encloses, surrounds and moves him. It is the horizon that his existence can realize only by journeying towards it; as he journeys, the mystery gets closer, but as it gets closer, it appears to be further away, so that man appears to reach the limits of what is possible, as if he has not yet been created, and his profound desire for death, that is, for birth, comes from this.

Nothing arouses man or makes him move or pushes him to go beyond his limits except his similarity (to God). This similarity, which brings man and God together, is the image. The image with regard to God is an unknown, which cannot be attained by knowing, and with regard to man is a known thing, which lights up the unknown for him. It excites our desire, but it escapes our understanding. Oneness cannot be achieved between man and the image, nor between resemblance and what is resembled, but it can be achieved between man and what transcends him, between what is limited and what is not limited, between the overt and the hidden, which remains hidden. Man cannot become one except with the unknown, which remains unknown. This union is like the falling of a droplet of water into an endless river, for it is not the union of limit with limit, or body with body, or thing with thing.

If man understands the image, which is similar to him, he can go on to understand the meaning, and become one with what is not similar to him. He must be limited in order to improve his chances of attaining what is limitless. He comes from soil, which he must leave in order to rejoin it. To reveal the meaning is to reveal man in this universe: fragility and change. It is as if man can achieve eternity only by destroying time, and he can only settle in a place that he leaves.

9

Ibn 'Arabi analyses the relationship between meaning and image, literally. He points out that the *kaf* (the k) in kun (universe) is a shadow of the word 'be' (*k-n*), 'the command of God', because this word (*k-n*) is the essence, whose shadow is the universe (*kun*), and that the *waw* (u) in *huwa* (he) refers to the existence of the image in us, which means that the h in *huwa* (he) is a symbol of the essence, and the *waw* is a symbol of divine revelation, i.e. the symbol of the universe. When we write w a w (*waw alif waw*) the way that we pronounce it (*waw*), Ibn 'Arabi describes the first letter *waw* as the *waw* in *huwiya* (identity), the second letter *waw* as the *waw* contained in *kun* (universe) and the *alif* (a) as the veil of oneness that separates them (*Kitab al-Mim wal-Waw wal-Nun*, pp. 9–10).

Divine revelations symbolize image as 'she' (*hiya*). For *hiya* is *huwa* but *huwa* is not *hiya* (she is he but he is not she.) Image is meaning, but meaning is not image. Ibn 'Arabi says that 'he' is not 'she', and when 'he' becomes 'she', it is 'only to create the image' (simile), and 'he' is the action (verb) and 'she' is the receiver, and the 'h' is the command that unites 'he' and 'she', the reason that links two prefaces. When 'he' is, there is nothing with him, and 'he' in the sense of he does not have an existence, and 'she' in the sense of she does not have an existence. And the 'h' in the sense of h does not have an existence, for the 'h' moves the 'he' and the 'she', and the 'he' and the 'she' meet through the 'h', and existence happens. So this meeting of 'he' and 'she' is referred to by the two letters that make up *k-n* (be). When we want something, we say to it: 'Be, and it is', and the thing here is the 'she' and our wish is the 'he' and what we say is 'h' and '*k-n*' (be) is the reason of the linkage, and the 'k' from *k-n* is the 'he' and the 'n' from *k-n* is the 'she'.

Ibn 'Arabi goes on to say, 'As the *waw* is supreme, we have made it the husband, and the 'he' is male. The 'she' is supreme because of her influence but lower because of the *kasra* (the 'i'), so we have given it a '*ya*' (y) and we have made it *al-ahl* (family). In this case, the 'h' is the message and the 'he' is like Gibril. The rules and the laws and the states and the mysteries appear from this blessed union (*Kitab al-Ya*', p. 11).

# 10

The writings of Sufis such as al-Niffari, al-Tawhidi and Ibn 'Arabi shed light on three characteristics of this school of writing, which was the force behind the change in Arab poetical writing.

First: poetry is not a linguistic game, in which words are ornamental and decorative tools, and play no active or ideative role. On the contrary, poetry is something that transcends the form. It is emotion and action at the same time. It is the way the human being feels and thinks, the way he understands things and the way he relates to them. It is a kind of consciousness, and because of that it is, by necessity, a kind of thought. As matter or meaning converge in the poem, emotions and meaning are also drawn together.

Second: what we call external, material or natural reality is only one aspect of existence, and its most restricted. What we call life or existence has a broader scope. Poets who limit their interest and their expression to the external aspect are ultimately only interested in what they are presenting to everyone, and therefore express only what everyone knows. Their position can be traced back to naturalism, which sees only the branches, leaves and fruit of a tree, rather than the internal movement of its roots, sap and growth. However, what is behind nature is only another part of nature.

Third: what we call truth does not exist in the world of phenomena apart from in its scientific-conventional form. The truth, on the contrary, is mystery, hidden inside things, in their concealed world. Man is able to reach it only with specific knowledge, which is neither conventional nor 'scientific'. Opposite the visible in the world arises the invisible and opposite the objective in the world arises the subjective.

However, going beyond the formal game, external reality and natural overt appearances demand a radical change in the ways of acquiring knowledge, which will bring about complete emancipation from the stranglehold of the social-religious political establishment and what it has written or marginalized and will lead to the freeing up of the internal subjective dynamic of the world with its emotions and desires and dreams, with its unconscious, natural instincts and aspirations and things it suppresses and everything that the culture of the body requires, which goes beyond the culture of the 'spirit' in its religious forms, in particular.

If the apparent culture as defined by the socio-political religious establishment is limited and it is easy to limit it, then the inner culture is not limited and it is difficult to limit it. If the language that explains the former is limited and restrictive like it, then the language that explains the latter is not limited and escapes any form of limitation. Thus we name the first language logical, direct, clear, and we name the second, affective, obscure, figurative. The first computes and represents things and the second awakens and enriches them.

## 11

Sufi writing is the experience of attaining the absolute and it is what we find among the great creators in all ages. Myth and symbol are two forms that direct us towards greater depths and broader horizons and a more certain search for meaning. They are one of the ways of returning to the collective unconscious, to what goes beyond the individual, to human memory and its fables, to the past as a kind of unconsciousness – they are all a symbol, which goes beyond the relative to the absolute. To explain it poetically, ideas do not appear by themselves, as in philosophy, but appear only in their relationships with what is within them.

Symbol and myth are the meeting point between the apparent and the concealed, the visible and the invisible. They are therefore the point of illumination, the dynamic centre, which is diffused in all directions. At the same time, they are expressions of different levels of all kinds of reality. This is what allows the poet not only to discover what we do not know, but also to re-create what we know, since he links it with the movement of the unknown and the unending. On this level, poetry becomes knowledge.

# 12

But what is symbol in Arab poetry? It means a sign and a sign is one way of indicating meaning. Al-Jahiz says that the sense of what something means can be conveyed, not only through literal, but also through figurative means. It is a quick, covert and indirect indication.

Qudamah Bin Ja'far refers to symbolism as follows: 'A speaker uses a symbol in his speech when he wishes to conceal [its meaning] from everyone and inform only some of them about it. He gives the word or letter, the name of a bird, a wild animal or some other species or a letter of the alphabet and tells only those whom he wishes to understand what he has done; thus it is an expression that can be understood by them and concealed in symbols from everyone else. The books of previous philosophers and wise men demonstrate a great use of symbol, and Plato was among the strongest of them in the use of symbols. In the Qur'an, there are symbols for great and serious things. They include the knowledge of what will happen and the use of letters of the alphabet and different oaths, such as the fig and olive and dawn and time and sun. Those who are knowledgeable in the science of the Qur'an know their exact meanings (*Naqdat al-nathr*, pp. 61–62). Qudamah Ibn Ja'far says about *ishara* (allusion) that it is a concise form, indicating that the symbol is also an abbreviation. He defines it by saying that it is a few words that contain many meanings that refer to it, or it is a quick flash, which suggests such meanings (*Naqd al-sh'ir*, p. 9). The symbol according to this definition is an indicative flash.

Ibn Rashiq, developing the concept of the symbol/allusion says that the allusion is 'an indicative flash used in all kinds of speech, which is a precise intimation, which informs the whole and whose meaning is very different from its literal expression' (al-'Umda, p. 206:1).

Al-Qushayri describes Sufi writers as 'employing expressions among themselves, by which they intend to reveal the meanings to themselves, and hide and conceal the explanation from those who oppose their beliefs. They make the meanings of such expressions unintelligible to foreigners/non-Sufis as they are jealous lest their secrets will be spread among those who are not part of them, because their knowledge is not obtained by different methods, rather God, the most high, has placed it in the hearts of certain people and has selected those people to understand the real meaning of this knowledge (Risalat al-Qushayria, Cairo, Bulaq Press, 1984 AH, p. 40).

The basis of symbol in the Arab language lies in its brevity and distance between the implicit and explicit meanings of the words. The poet therefore does not explain or make clear but rather, as al-Buhtari says, only provides a flash, whose indication is enough. Understanding requires interpretation. It is by its nature obscure. Abu Ishaq al-Sabi says, 'The most noble of poetry is the most obscure, and gives up its intention only after some delay' (al-Mathl al-Sair, vol. 2, p. 414). Al-Jurjani says, 'It is a fact of nature that something that has been sought after and longed and yearned for will be sweeter and more excellent when it is obtained, and it will be of more value and of greater worth to the person, who will be more consumed and enamoured with it (Asrar al-Balagha, p. 118). He distinguishes between ambiguity and complexity. He says, 'Complexity in poetry and speech is not only blameworthy because it requires thought in the sentence but also because the writer makes your thoughts stumble by doing this, and makes the path to meaning so difficult and hard to walk upon, that maybe he will divide your mind, and confuse your thinking, so that you won't know where to start from and how to seek the meaning' (Asrar al-Balagha, p. 125).

Mallarmé says no more than this when he talks about the obscurity of poetry. In all cases, poetry appears as the great creators practise it as a movement towards knowing the unknown – the culture of the body taking precedence over the culture of reason, and spontaneity and innate sense taking precedence over logic and analysis – and this is itself what Surrealist writing endorses.

## 13

It is possible to describe the experience of writing, the experience of the writer as an experience of death in the Sufi sense of the word: death of the social external world with its different levels and relationships, for the sake of life in the universal internal world. Therefore, writing has to transcend the apparent and demolish it. It has to go beyond the language of the transparent and demolish it. One of the signs of decay in poetic writing in the modern world is the supremacy of literal language – the supremacy of tradition and terms.

We transcend the world of the apparent with the language itself: we intoxicate it. We must create a delirium in the language, which corresponds to the delirium of experience. It is true to say that every Sufi writer aspires to discover 'the universal language', which expresses the correspondence between what is infinite (meaning) and what is finite (image). This language speaks without the intervention of reason. It is a language that dazzles the reader – it transports him to the infinite. And as the Sufi is 'intoxicated', his language is intoxicated as well. He creates a particular delirium for the language within his delirium. He expresses man's delirium through delirious language. The language must come out of itself, in the same way as the Sufi comes out from himself.

This intoxicated language is the language of metaphor (figurative speech). This language enables someone who is elsewhere in the abstract or concealed world to cross over into our world – the apparent. This language permits us to place the infinite in the finite, as Baudelaire says.

This mystery, the infinite, the unknown, is not a point we can reach and at which knowledge ends. On the contrary, it is moveable – each time we discover something about it, the things that demand to be known increase. It is not possible to arrive at a complete understanding of the mystery.

Thus the language, however delirious it is, does not establish 'true' relationships between the self and the other, the self and the mystery, the self and the universe – but establishes only figurative relationships.

## 14

Figurative language, according to the Sufi experience, is a bridge that links the visible to the invisible, the known to the mysterious. As the goal is to reveal the unknown, so the image, strictly speaking, is only a particular invention. It is therefore not a simile, produced by comparison or analogy, but a figure of speech, produced by bringing two distant worlds close together and conjoining them – so that they become one. Therefore, the image is not an artificial or a technical way of expression, in other words, it is not explanatory or rhetorical, but it is primordial. It bursts forth with the same force as poetical intuition. The power of the image and its richness lie in the type of relationships that it creates or reveals, between these two worlds – and which it leaves, at the same time as it is unable to gather them rationally, i.e. unable to domesticate and make them conform to perceptible reality. They are real since they reveal essential origins, but at the same time, they escape from tangible reality since they allude to what transcends it. Therefore they are not descriptive, but they are like a light that penetrates and reveals; they are a way towards the unknown. In this sense, they generate shock and summon up a new sensitivity. This helps us understand how poetry in the Sufi experience is not literary in the conventional sense of the word, but it is an enquiry into the essence of man and existence, and a desire to change the image of the world; in brief, it is a re-fashioning of man and existence. The image here is a transfer – it transcends and changes.

This takes us on to dream, vision, *shath* and madness, which in the poetical Sufi experience represent a means of expression, another form of language, contained within the language, which helps to reveal man and existence in a deeper, richer and more complete way. As a means of discovery, they form a way of understanding truths that cannot be understood logically or rationally. Reason and logic know only perceptible things or the abstract, and therefore the images that emanate from them are non-evocative, because they distinguish between the visible and the invisible, while the figurative images of Sufism bring together the tangible and the abstract, the apparent and the concealed, the known and the unknown. The image in Sufi figurative language is not an isolated part in a sentence or an expression, and it does not originate out of a desire to embellish or to persuade and provoke, which leaves us on the surface of reality, but is an organic part of every macrocosm: images are people and places and subjects and events and actions. They link us to symbol and myth, because they originate from this ascending, descending dialectic, between God and man, between invisible reality and visible reality. They are charged with dreams and irrational elements such as magic and hallucinations and madness and *shath* and ecstasy.

In Sufi experience, the unseen, the mystery, is the most profound, because it is the origin. Therefore trying to understand what is visible is only trying to understand the superficial and external. The soul is not superficial, but extends endlessly in depth and breadth. The value of the expression lies in the extent to which it reveals this scope and its relationships – in the extent to which it reveals the infinite dimension, in man and the world.

This constant movement of discovering the infinite contains a continuous demolition of forms, or it has not been fixed in form. That is because form, like image, in this movement is a pure invention, which is not manufactured or borrowed. It is not a covering or a wrap or a receptacle: it is a space. It is the manner and process of our thoughts. It is a structure of relationships between words. In essence, the apparent in figurative language is not what speaks but the inner meaning, the image is not what writes but rather the meaning. The Sufi is the other, the objective other in figurative language, at the moment he is subjective, and because of that he is not the one who speaks in meaning and writes in the image; rather, the meaning is what makes him speak and write. He is not the one who thinks and writes; rather, he is the one who is thought about and who is written about: one thinks me, as Rimbaud said at a later time.

## 15

The Sufi creates an allegorical world with the force of his metaphor and language, which is a world that is perceptible and known through imagination, which can be lived as a world of events that belong in particular to inner history. This relationship between the inner and the outer, the concealed and the apparent, is the most profound source of vision of internal acts, and it is a relationship that resembles a two-sided mirror. This relationship is the fusion of things that are perceptible with those that are not, since the one-dimensional exterior does not become the only authority in which psychological and spiritual acts lie.

This relationship becomes the essence itself of creative imagination among the Sufis.

Thus creative imagination, which is the place of exchange, the place in which the perceptible and the imperceptible intersect, epitomizes the macrocosm, i.e. the entire universe in the microcosm – man.

Creative imagination makes the body transparent, since it itself becomes the other world that Sufi gnosis attains. The body becomes an element for generating the imaginative structure of the place, and becomes a Sufi dimension and song of the interior, which reflects upon the exterior place, restructuring it in its image. Poetry in this sense is the imaginative dimension that restructures the exterior world in the image of its creator, the internal world.

The Sufi develops the macrocosm in his body, which is the microcosm – in such a manner that he makes his body live, after it has become transparent, through the action of the creative imagination itself as the original, the primordial domain of what is possible.

The microcosm (the body) as the place of life, like the drawings of imagination, becomes the precedent of the place, the universe. The universe preserves the close links with the imaginary place of the translucent body.

The body, as a place of life, basically and fundamentally brings together the allegoric and the material in its figurative form. Man represents the union of the allegoric and the material, and thus the body is the domain of the possible, a place in which what is perceptible by the senses can be transformed.

This reflection of the internal to the external is itself the transfer of present knowledge: in this knowledge, which is the product of imaginative knowledge, are revealed the 'mysteries' of the universe, and they are the gnostic discoveries, which conventional knowledge is unable to reach.

The world of allegory as far as the Sufis are concerned does not refer to an empty or fantastical world, but reveals a real world deeply rooted at the heart of the world of appearances. In the world of allegory, the spirit takes physical form and the physical takes spiritual form in what can be seen only with the eye of the imagination. Here the Sufi becomes his essence and his 'otherness' at the same time. The contradictions are obliterated. The tangible/perceptible world becomes the presence of the one (God). The real and the figurative meet and become one in imaginary forms, which reveal what is happening internally. The poeticality of Sufi writing springs out of this mystical singularity and becomes itself the transforming erotic language: 'every pulse beat in me bears the trace of the beloved, and in every atom of my body, the beloved talks' (Jalal al-Din al-Rumi). Thus it brings alive the world and everything that exists in it like divine revelation of the One. There is no existence outside the One.

Inside this singularity, the low is not incompatible with the high. In this, we understand the end of contradictions or the supreme point of Surrealism.

This gnosis is completely free of any ready-made elements, and is not determined in advance by any rational controls. Imaginative-perceptive (cognitive) understanding is perception of things in their entirety and in their primordial-original forms. It is the place in which gnosis develops, which cannot be described; it is words that cannot be said. It is therefore broader than objective perception. For such perception is subject to mathematical limitations of time and quantitative limitations of place and gives us only a partial and superficial knowledge of things.

In creative imagination, therefore, the perceptible and the imperceptible are transformed: the first rises and the second sinks. This is the dialectic of the meeting between physical love and spiritual love, from which is born Sufi love. This love reaches a state of higher existence and higher consciousness: the lover becomes one with the beloved in a limitless love. The Sufi feels that he is liberated: he comes out of himself, out of the natural and sensory limitations. (He comes out of himself to enter himself in a more profound and distant way.)

The experience of love is therefore the experience of knowledge (love is knowledge), which reveals the mysteries of the universe to the Sufi. With love, the heart becomes the eye with which he contemplates the One; in the same way, thought becomes a light, which illumines inner sight. For love is also, like gnosis, the starting point of experience and its means and its goal.

Thus we see that delirium, which the cult of love produces in the Sufi's soul, is a kind of universal consciousness or awareness; it is a consciousness that generates a radiance with which man lives on another level of existence (the oneness of existence), since he appears to be a member of a human society of another kind. In addition to this state of creative and supreme delirium and joy and intoxication, there is a state that cannot be described. These can all be compared to an everlasting and eternal intuition.

On this level, Sufism is 'a religion of love', as Ibn 'Arabi says. In this sense, it changes the meaning of identity.

# 16

Identity, according to prevailing cultural opinion, is an ambiguous entity, and the other exists for it only inasmuch as it relinquishes its own identity and changes into it – it melts into its I-ness. This comes about either by the self dissolving into the other or by the self repudiating the other and making it separate. This makes the universe a storeroom in which what is repudiated and eliminated is amassed, so it creates on a human level a spurious universality, a universality of master and slave, repudiator and repudiated, and creates on a historical level a universality of exploitation and consumerist technology and on the level of civilization a universality of similarity, which annihilates freedom and creativity.

We must emerge from this identity if we are to take our true place in the universe. I have found no better or more profound way than Sufism of showing us how to do that.

Identity, according to this experience, is constantly open (to the other). The self is a constant movement towards the other. In order for the self to reach the other, it must go beyond itself. To put it another way, the self travels towards its profound essence only when it travels towards the other and its profound essence, and, in the other, the self will find the most perfect presence. The I, on the contrary, is the non-I. From this point of view, identity, like love, is continuously being created. Thus the Sufi says, when he is at his most aware, I am not I. Rimbaud echoes this in his own way: 'I is the other.' In other words, it is as if the Sufi and Rimbaud are speaking with one tongue. I am, I live, I think – therefore I am the other, I am not I.

17

The Sufi experience teaches us that when the self expresses the truth or what we think of as the truth, it does not speak of it exhaustively, in fact, it does not speak of it directly, but only alludes to it, or refers to it in symbols. For the truth is not in what is said, in what it is possible to say, but rather it is in what is not said, or in what it is difficult to say. It lies in the obscure, the concealed, the unending. The Sufi experience is the continuation of a deep-rooted gnostic tradition, which believes that fortunately man is not able to understand the mystery of man and the universe. This tradition goes back to Gilgamesh, who saw everything, so he saw that the truth was not in what he saw and understood, but rather in what he could not see and understand, and from there it can be traced to the traditions of Hermes and Eleusis.

Perhaps this is what compels Sufis to practise extremism – to work to transform the body into a dynamic tide, by rendering ineffective the senses and reason, in order to attain the unknown – the infinite. Rimbaud and the Surrealists would go on to adopt this practice later. Thus the body becomes an ecstatic, radiant entity, and the matter becomes diaphanous, and the obstacles between man and the unknown or the 'true and absent life' vanish.

Language and life, the self and the other appear through the relationship with this invisible unknown, as figurative language and figurative dialectic, and thus the I becomes the other, and the individual self does not speak, but rather the macro, universal self, contained in it does. The self does not speak in this macro-creative moment, but the essence itself becomes the subject – since it is the other and the universe, or since the macrocosm is contained in it.

Naming, writing things on a universe level, means enquiring into the core, the illuminated, the very near, the very far, that which I call the absent place, 'the macro world'.

This world is not abstract, nor is it separate. It is the here and now incorporated into what Pascal calls 'the thinking reed' – man.

In it the general universal is no more than private individuality, in its repletion and its specificity. The universe from this theory is the globe – the communal dome in which different creations embrace each other.

# The Harmonious Difference

Hide me from my name, or I saw him and he didn't see me.
*al-Niffari*

Every name has names.
*al-Niffari*

1

Whether Sufism is regarded as pious or heretical, there is no doubt that its ideas and writings represent a gnostic upheaval in the history of Arab-Islamic thought. It has not been the aim of this research to carry out an in-depth study of the development and origins of this experience, nor the political, social and economic conditions that surround it – about which many books have been written – but only to consider it from its texts. To put it another way, it has not been my objective to study Sufism as an occurrence but rather as an art form.

2

Who decides what the correct meaning of the text of the Qur'an should be? This is the issue that lies at the heart of the dispute or battle between those who believe in subjective experience and the objective establishment, between the Sufi and the theologian, the text itself becoming the battleground.

In reading and interpretation, the Sufi goes beyond the literal meaning of the text to its inner significance. While the orthodox *shari'a* relies on literal meaning, the Sufi goes beyond it to the truth. Thus the Sufi interprets the text of the Qur'an in such a manner as to create a cosmic space that is broad enough for his vast experience, and through which he reveals the dynamic nature of the text and its inner riches.

However, this manner of interpretation has had severe repercussions on those who interpret the text literally, which has led to an upheaval in the ideas based on it with regard to theology and religious law. In this upheaval, the authority that was founded upon it has also undergone a major change.

In this joint endeavour between orthodox theology, on the one hand, and political authority, on the other, the literal interpreters are driven by their need to maintain religion, to think and behave as if they have a monopoly on the text of the Qur'an, the text of revelation, and possess it exclusively. In reality, this merely represents a need to preserve the dominant authority and its culture. With that in mind, they begin to regard anyone who does not hold similar opinions to them and share their understanding of the meaning of the text as an opponent and someone who is working to wrest that possession away from them. Therefore let him be blamed, let him be described as a heretic, a sinner, an atheist and unbeliever. This is what has helped transform Arab Islamic society into one that ostracizes, isolates and repudiates anyone who doesn't share its views, and which is exclusive and murderous. The literalists use the text of the Qur'an itself to justify these measures. They have transformed the text; it has become the centre of a power struggle, rather than an arena in which people compete to study and reveal its ideological dimensions. The literalists not only kill their enemies, but they also kill the text itself, since they restrict it to its canonical role, which is subject to the rule of reason in the way it is interpreted and applied.

3

The Sufi experience as 'heretical doctrine' (*bid'a*) is a measure that enables us to discover the nature of established religious thought and its like. It permits the researcher to study the manner in which Arab-Islamic society defined itself, and the way in which it excluded the other within it. It also permits us to consider the dynamic of heresy (*bid'a*) and its changing role inside the dominant ruling order. However, this lies outside the field of our research, though I hope other researchers will undertake a study of it. I have been content with studying this experience from the point of view of literary heresy, as I have pointed out. This allows me to look beyond Sufism to the literary experience of Surrealism, which is also regarded as heretical in the history of Western literature.

4

The Sufi experience as 'literary heresy' goes beyond the framework of religion, in the literal or established sense of the word. It is an experience that reveals the inner, invisible world and expresses it. It is a search for the truth, contained in the inner, invisible world, and which emerges from a state that transcends theological or legalistic reasoning, which is based on the literal meaning of the Qur'an. A legalistic interpretation is finite because it is linked to the world, but truth is infinite because it is linked to the secret of the divine – the secret of the universe.

This infinite 'truth' resists expression or can be expressed only through symbols, signs and signals. Thus in Sufi writing, the universe appears as a house inhabited by symbols, indications and allusions, a house in which everything in it is borrowed from truth – the infinite mystery.

Although the Sufi writes in the same language as everyone

else, like the poet, he uses it in a different way and makes it say something different. He places the words in a space with which they are unfamiliar and from here goes on to use them to create a beauty that is unknown.

5

How does the Sufi experience relate to that of the Surrealists? How can we compare them? What is the basis that gives this comparison an ideative or cultural legitimacy?

First of all, I should point out that in attempting to answer these questions I have looked at the Sufi experience as a spiritual, ideative path and not as a religious belief. Starting from that, it is possible to say that the Sufi experience has had a unique significance for people who wish to free themselves from a material world, which feels as if it is enchaining them. For it is an experience that links man to his inner self, and transcends the real world, which veils man from this self. The Surrealist experience is similar to the Sufi experience. It rids mankind of his sense of estrangement or the sense of absence he feels in this material world. On this level it appears to be a form of Sufism. This is particularly apparent in its distinctive use of language, to establish fields and signs and an atmosphere that entirely resembles that which the Sufi experience establishes. It is an experience that goes beyond familiar ways of approaching reality, and guides us to what is further away and richer. To put it another way, it smashes the obstructive ruin that familiar reality represents. It is a force that rejects prevailing ideas and pushes towards something that is better and more beautiful. Just as the language of Sufism reexamines the prevailing orthodox language (the literal), by going beyond it to establish an original language (a figurative language), so the Surrealist experience reexamines the prevailing language (the fixed, the classical) to establish an original language (transformation, creativity). The sublime, the inner world, the secret, the unseen, the unnamed are all aspects of Sufism, which can be compared to aspects of Surrealist belief such as the supernatural, the unconscious and the unknown, which is not perceived in its entirety but which appears to be pushing us to discover more, each time a part of it is revealed. Just as the Sufi experience transcends the established religious cultural order, the Surrealist experience also goes beyond the dominant established socio-cultural order. Just as this life provides the Sufi with the basis for what he lives and sees, the Surrealist also bases his vision on his experience of life. Trance is the first state that the Sufi lives, and illumination the second state that the Surrealist lives. Both words have the same meaning. The Sufi inhabits the invisible and the Surrealist the unknown; the fundamental goal of both people is to experience revelation, which will help them in their desire to go to the furthest point. Going to the furthest point fulfils a wish or a need in them to change the prevailing ways of seeing and knowing. In Surrealism, this leads the artist to create an unfamiliar image, which startles the ordinary reader, and in Sufism, to create something that is unacceptable to the orthodox view. Such states of creativity are called delirium or unconsciousness, in the first instance, and *shath*, in the second. In both cases, the nature of the Sufi and Surrealist experience is irrational and cannot be understood rationally. This is because it comes from a state that lies beyond the state of reason, as the Sufi says. Therefore the aim of this experience is to free the conscious self from the ties that bind it to everyday life and raise it to another 'transcendental' life.

At this level, every true poet is Sufi or Surrealist: he longs for something beyond the familiar world, and is conscious that he will not be able to achieve it unless he fulfils two conditions: first, to rid himself completely of any traces of the established poetical climate, in order to purify himself and his language; second, to allow himself to be carried away with this new-found purity, to a language and world that are unfamiliar to him. Only in such a way will the poem reveal something that we have not seen before. It does not mean that it will be unreal – rather, it means that it will present reality from a different angle: not linked to visible reality, but in conjunction with it in some other form. The reality that will be revealed through this poem will be more realistic than direct visible reality – through the exhausted appearance of reality, the *qasida* will reveal an unknown inner sense of reality. This demonstrates the effective power of the poem, i.e. its ability to change our familiar methods of knowledge and life.

Surrealism, like Sufism, starts off by rejecting the limitations imposed on the human condition, and therefore lives through dreams and the unconscious world, in a confusion of the senses, which it expresses through what it calls automatic writing, i.e. writing that is completely uncensored by reason or conscious thought. It is an experience that attempts to bypass the customary for the virginal and the unfamiliar and to go beyond the contradictions of thought and life – by changing life and man. Surrealism remains, however, an 'external' stance, compared to Sufism, i.e. it remains a form of inquisitive consciousness, whereas Sufism represents the extinction of individual consciousness. It is, as al-Bastami says, 'a detachment from the self' and from everything that is 'external'.

Surrealism, like Sufism, does not merely aspire to argue about writing, but aims to go further than that, by enlarging the field of writing and work, and freeing the stifled power of the unconscious self or the unknown in man and by returning to man everything he possesses – everything that he is able to think and dream about.

Their belief that poetry has the power to change man and reveal truths is derived from their belief that man is the starting point of truth and wisdom and that the universe is a form of experience like a subjective desire.

According to Surrealism, therefore, poetry frees man from the technical limitations of belief and reveals that one thing has many and varied meanings, which in turn demonstrate the fragility of the dominant perspective and the poverty of the material vision of the world. Like Sufism, it also works to push back both the boundaries of the conscious world and those of knowledge, bringing about, through the former, a new harmony between the forces of wakefulness and the forces of the dream and, through the latter, a new harmony between forces of the apparent, external world and the forces of the concealed, inner world.

6

To achieve such a harmony, the Sufis enjoin the rejection of the religious and legislative establishment and its values, and the Surrealists the rejection of the socio-religious establishment and its values.

In both cases this rejection is only the first step in the search for the 'supreme point', the point of 'the unity – oneness'; this 'point' has no fixed locus, by which I mean that it is not limited by place, and escapes normal detection. It is the 'point' of the beginning/the end, the origin/the return, the manifest/the concealed. It can be found in the geography of the imagination, and can be perceived only through the imagination.

According to the Sufis and the Surrealists, to attain this point is to attain one's origins and realize the oneness of being. This attainment is achieved by transforming the sensory-psychic powers and controlling them, in one way or another, so that the power of imagination is revealed. At this stage, the body becomes tractable and equipped with extraordinary powers; it is a limitless space, in which man can see himself through his body and be conscious of it as a micro-world, which contains a macro-world. The invisible world becomes his heart, and the universe, his body. He is a 'complete' man who bears a universal message.

Initially, man is estranged and lives in exile far away from this point. His true life is absent. Attainment of this point is a gnostic and existential presence, which transcends exile. Sufi writing, like surrealist writing, is the story of his emergence from exile and attainment of this point.

The reaching of this point, for the Sufi, can be described as the emergence from 'occidental exile', as Suhrawardi put it, and for the

Surrealists, the emergence from mechanistic and religious values – that other 'occidental exile'.

Both Sufism and Surrealism clearly demonstrate how the life of man is an adventurous journey, which takes him from his present false life to his absent true life. There are two stages to this journey – consciousness of interior exile – the I, the exiled, on the one hand – and, on the other, sinking into the soul, into the depths of the self.

The 'occidental exile' of Suhrawardi is a blessing that lights up this adventure. The journey takes place between two spots: the place of exile, outside the 'point' that Suhrawardi termed the 'east', the world of light, and the place of captivity, in the 'west', the world of darkness. There are three stages to the journey: in the first stage, the person is held in captivity, in a place in which there are chains, deep empty prisons and layers of darkness, piled one on top of another. For the Surrealists, this stage is represented by daily life, the life of technology, religion and traditions. The second stage consists of escape towards the east, i.e. 'the supreme point', and the third stage is the attainment of the source of life (unity of being/the supreme point).

The Sufi is searching for his self, and the 'source of life' is only his true self. It is the conscious, complete self. Realizing this higher self is conditional on the transformation of the I, the separated part of the self, which lives as 'alien'. At the end of the journey, the exile will end and the Sufi will become one, a perfect man. He will achieve oneness, the oneness of essence between this perfect man and the only existence: the self (the I) becomes the he, i.e. God.

The 'east', 'the supreme point', cannot be attained except through punishment in the 'west'. For the search for the 'east' (the true, supernatural life) is a form of exploration and excavation into the depths of the self, where it concludes by going beyond the I, wandering in the external world and dissolving into the essence and understanding it.

Thus it completes the ontological revolution within the self. It is a 'revolution of the heart', a revolution that reveals the secret, the veiled. It is the revolution of 'oneness'.

I said that Surrealist writing, like Sufi writing, is the story of emergence from exile, and movement towards the 'supreme point'. Such writing is realized in Sufism as *shath* and in Surrealism as automatic writing. It is distinguished by the complete lack of any rational, aesthetic, moral, religious or socio-political censure. Thus, it is an outburst from the inner world, which is usually stifled by these many forms of censorship. It says everything that cannot be said and everything that cannot be conveyed. Because of that, it convulses speech and the system of speech. By revealing the infinity of man's inner nature through his faculties, it has led to an overthrow of both the spoken and the material order.

Writing is no longer a tool, but becomes an activity of the human essence and a spoken revelation. Writing becomes an extension of the spiritual and physical essence. Therefore, it is possible for us to say: writing is the thing. The question now is not: 'to what extent is it artistically beautiful?' but rather: 'to what extent is it laden with meaning, sense and revelation?' It is a form of writing that raises questions not about literature but about the meaning of existence and man. It reveals man's inner world, his madness in attempting to attain this world, his delirium and hallucinations and his sense of being lost and going astray. It is a form of journey from an obscure land to an unknown other. It is concerned with man, as a whole, and not some aesthetic theory or rational view, or feelings and emotions by themselves.

It is a form of writing that is searching for knowledge and a way of deliverance. It makes man rise above himself or pushes him to reach outside himself.

First, it is a way of ridding man of the chains of censorship that society imposes or that the material world of the senses enjoins, as well as ridding him of what is prohibited and what is suppressed and prevented so that he can embrace freedom and live it.

It is a form of writing that crosses the divide between dream and reality by the bridge of desire.

Finally, I should like to raise the question about the relationship between science, on the one hand, and Sufism and Surrealism, on the other, although I will only touch on the subject and not go into it in depth, for that is outside the remit of our presentation.

It seems to me that Surrealism, like Sufism, is concerned with something that lies outside the reach of science. It does not necessarily contradict science, but supplements it in areas where it is weak, as if, in so doing, it is another independent science.

Both Sufism and Surrealism are not rediscovering beauty in things so much as revealing new secrets in man and universe, so from this point of view they belong to science.

Sufism developed at a stage when traditional religious studies and rational science were flowering in Arab society, in the same way as Surrealism developed at the time when an enormous scientific revolution in the West was taking place in physics and mathematics.

Just as Sufism opened up the field of Arab-Islamic culture to a study of metaphysics and life, which science had failed to do, Surrealism did the same in Western culture.

Following on from this, we can describe Sufism as being a radical rejection of both traditional and rational lore, which introduced man subsequently to many and varied areas that he had traditionally been forbidden to enter or been dissuaded from looking at or writing about. Sufism, in that way, was a yardstick for modern writing. It is impossible to assess any artistic or ideative Arab output of any significance at all without looking at the extent to which it has been submerged in these areas.

Surrealism represents a similar contribution to Western cultural output.

The final issue that I wish to mention in this context concerns psychoanalysis as a science. Psychoanalysis has provided a basis by which it has become possible to explain Sufi and Surrealist texts in detail and to reveal their meaning. It has thus given Sufism and Surrealism a scientific validity, as both of them are important sources of knowledge, and as the work that originates from them is an important metaphysical document.

# PART TWO

# The Visible Invisible

*Followed by*
## Four Studies

# The Writings of al-Niffari
## or the Poetic of Thought

1

It is a literary experience that begins by breaking away from reality and forming a link with the imaginary – or with the potentiality of reality. It is an experience that goes beyond reality, in order to plunge into it and examine its secrets in detail.

It is an experience of symbols, signs and allusions. There is more to the text than the explicit meaning of the words. It is intersected by dimensions and meanings that embody a language, which assumes a connection with it through experience or intuition. The text is a language, which not only conveys the secrets of imaginary things but also the mysteries of the essence.

The text is doubly estranged, from both poetic writing of the time and the language in which it is written. It lies outside the norms of poetical and cultural practice. It practises other ways of seeing, writing and expression and forms different links between language and the thing, between the name and what is named, and thereby overturns the conventional literary system. Thus this text, coming as it does from the unknown, confronts us with the need to read it as a reference for itself. It is necessary to read it with the eye of the heart, not in the light of the known but in the light of the unknown.

## 2

Al-Niffari's work is characterized by his departure from the established system of signs, meanings, images, etc that had been used by previous writers to denote things (things that were named). Al-Niffari writes in an abstruse way hitherto unknown. He extracts things from their past, from the meanings they had before and the ways in which they were expressed and places them in new images to which he applies new names. Writing is changing here. It is giving new meaning to objects since it is giving new meaning to the images in which they are used and the relationships in which they are involved; it is giving new meaning to language since it is developing new relationships between word and word and between words and objects. Al-Niffari has no preconceived notions of the meaning of words or the concept of the world. The world he writes about is neither determined nor defined: it does not have a ready-made identity, but one that appears to be constantly arriving and never ending. Man also appears to be similarly resistant to every ready-made and finite identity. Like the world, he is in flux, and he creates his identity out of the way he gives expression to the world. He creates his essence in the work he creates.

## 3

Thus it can be seen how the writings of al-Niffari do not examine the concrete external world because the word, in poetry, is not an instrument (it ceases to be poetical if it is nothing but an instrument), nor do they examine the allegoric external because the word, in poetry, is not seeking for inspiration (it ceases to be poetry if it has no inspiration). This writing examines the movement that allows the separation from the field that the names have already exhausted and allows communication with what has not been named, with the unseen. His examination is his constant movement in a space that does not end and which separates or continues to separate the words and things. His creativity lies in the manner in which he reveals the obscure relationships in the endless universe – which is infinitely obscure.

## 4

The writings of al-Niffari represent a rupture with the literary and cultural establishment. They are a radical reexamination of the theological–religious aspects of Arab culture in particular, and what they contain. His work sets up new relationships with the unknown, with the earth and sky, which challenge those relationships that have been firmly established by the religious-theological institutions. In addition, it creates another language for communicating with the unknown (God), which is different from the religious-theological language. It is not surprising, therefore, that al-Niffari's writings have convulsed the social-ideological order, which is more or less linked to the religious–theological vision. By so doing, they represent another dimension in writing and thought in Arab culture.

5

The Sufi experience has developed in a cultural climate, which is based on the belief that there is a single, unique and finite truth, and that everything else is false. This truth is embodied in the *shari'a* and the political order is based upon it and preserves it. Alternative forms of discourse are either compatible with it, in which case they are supererogatory, or contradictory, in which case they are rejected and repudiated.

The Sufis reject this simplification and go on to say that the orthodox, apparent truth does not represent the whole truth – for there exists a world to which orthodoxy does not refer, namely the absent and unknown or what they term the concealed inner truth. This concealed world cannot be reached by ways with which we are familiar in the manifest world, whether they are orthodox or rational, but it can be reached by other means, through the heart, intuition, illumination, vision … Knowledge of the truth (gnosis) in Sufism is thus linked to the knowing essence, in its particular experience, outside reason and tradition. As every essence has a different experience, so truth is revealed to each essence in a different form. But this difference is not a contradiction; on the contrary, it is rather an integration – or, to put it more correctly, plurality within one – the oneness of truth.

This difference means that expressing the essence of truth does not deplete it, since it does not speak it but rather alludes to it or symbolizes it. The truth does not lie in what is said or in what can be said, but is always in what is not said or in what it is difficult to say. It is always in the obscure, the concealed and the non-finite.

We know that the Sufi experience is a continuation of a deep-rooted gnostic tradition, which believes that man is unable to know what is secret, the mystery of man and things; this tradition goes back to Gilgamesh who 'saw everything' and who sees that the truth does not exist in what he knows but in what he does not know and can afterwards be found in the Hermes and Eleusis traditions.[1]

The Sufi experience goes further than that, in the way it treats poetical knowledge in particular, and attributes to it a dimension it has not had before. It is not content with rejecting reason as a concept. In fact, it nullifies it and the instruments it uses in the body. If man is to attain the infinite, he will have to change the body itself into a movable, unending tide, and he will achieve that only by destroying the action of the senses, as well as that of reason. This is an idea that Rimbaud and the Surrealists adopt about a thousand years later, when the entire body becomes a likeness for an ethereal being – the matter of ecstasy and illumination, in which there is no wall between it and the unknown, 'the true unseen life'.

So truth does not lie in what we are able to explain because elucidation is based on reason, but rather in what we are unable to explain or in what we are able to experience. Let us say: truth does not come from reason but is an experience of the heart.

6

The above demonstrates the problem that exists in dominant Arab culture, both today and in the past, of the essence in relation to the other and the essence in relation to the other outside this culture – i.e. the alien/foreign other.

This culture generates a form of recondite knowledge, which not only prevents an understanding of essence or identity but also prevents an understanding of the other. This culture eliminates the essence as a creative and changing power and regards it only as a vessel that contains teachings and ideas or as a conveyor of faith and custom.

The culture views identity as an impenetrable being; the other exists only by surrendering its own identity and becoming part of it – by melting into its I. It either glorifies the other in order to merge with it or it ridicules it in order to repudiate it and distance itself from it.

Perhaps the above goes some way to explaining the interest of creative Arabs today in the Sufi experiment in general and the writings of al-Niffari in particular and also helps to explain the attraction of visionary experience and illumination, the unknown, the mysterious and the absent, the unthinkable and what cannot be thought about and the mantled and the marginal – which all brings to mind the rich, pluralistic world that is created by this experience. In addition, it reminds us of the struggle of modern Arab writing to rid itself of socio-cultural constraints and analogies and to create new forms that are free from restrictive and set rules, as it sets out on its adventure of inquiring into and researching this universal unknown, seeking the invisible that the Sufi and the poet know will remain invisible.

We are made even more aware of the significance of this interest when we contemplate the different forms of obstruction that the Arab creator faces, particularly today, in the form of politics and religion. He lives and writes in a state of siege, inspired by a mystery, from which he begins to weave a hope, which will open up a horizon that will destroy the siege. He regards everything that is linked to the cultural, political, religious and theological reality to institutions and values, language and forms of writing as elements that intensify the severity of his siege and, accordingly, he regards everything that enables him to free himself from them as elements that will enable him to escape this state of siege. Therefore, the Sufi experiments in writing and culture appear like a single beacon of light, which illuminates the darkness of meaning and life. Poetry, like love, is a liberating work par excellence.

Al-Niffari raises this form of writing to a legendary level. His writing summons us to understand it. Our stomachs churn, our hearts thump as if we are melting into it, merging with it as we merge with our childhood and unconsciousness.

This form of writing is distinctive because ideas explode in a linguistic explosion. When the ideas escape from all forms of constraint, the language escapes as well; it frees both of them from their rational function and returns them to their basic task, which is to reveal the profundity of essence and the mysteries of existence. This eruption is filled with sudden changes and contrary tensions, in which the writing appears like a flood, flowing over the stage of the essence – it conveys, it changes, it mutates, without any apparent cause, as happens in a dream. In this flood, man seems troubled, longing, questioning: one moment he is longing for death, the next, clinging on to life like someone who never wants to die. The words also appear to be having an internal debate about what the world is discussing; it is as if al-Niffari has sewn them, then unravelled them stitch by stitch, then re-stitched them. He seems to be playing with essence and language and existence in a beautiful, glorious and fascinated movement, in a poetical language, that no one before him has been given. It is as if language itself is the movement of being, fused into a voice, into sounds and silences. Or it is as if it melts into the movement of experience. The idea is a complete poem and the poem is a complete thought.

Thus al-Niffari's writing takes us in to a world of promised infancy; or, rather, we can catch a glimpse of it through his poetry. It is the text of happiness, the text – the happiness. As we read it, we feel that we are escaping our tense conditions, since it closes the gap between the real world and the metaphysical, between man and the sacred, and dissolves the differences between man and God. It is a form of writing that tells us that truth is a longing and it exists only in complete clarity, i.e. in complete obscurity in language – I mean poetry.

8

Poetry provides us with the richest, most human and most beautiful link to the other world. For it is the most able to reveal the essence of the self and to disclose its other dimension. The self needs this other dimension not only to associate with, to match and to become one with, but also to provide it with a sense of its own uniqueness at the same time. The separateness of the other is what makes me clear to myself and brings me into harmony with it. Poetry brings together different individualities, constantly creating us in a universal human oneness. It takes us into a state of ecstasy, which is a state of waking sleep. In this sleep, which is the most perfect form of wakefulness, man works in brotherhood for the development of the world – to recall the expression of Heraclitus: 'Men, in their sleep, work fraternally for the development of the world.'

## 9

Nevertheless there remains the gnostic question par excellence, which can be expressed in the words of St Gregory Palamas: 'No word can hope for anything other than its own failure.' Since the language that we use to describe our essence and the other does not take us to the essence itself, how can we reach the other? The chasm, which appears behind it – the unknown, infinity – will never be filled. But does man possess a pledge that is more profound and more beautiful?

Let us compare the words of St Gregory to those of Leang-Kiai, one of the Tch'an masters, who says: 'We call an expression dead when its language still has language in it and we call an expression live when its language has no more language in it.'

If we look at the words of these two men today, they demonstrate that the writings of al-Niffari have a radiance about them that lights up modern Arabic writing in its struggle to free itself from 'dead expressions,' and they not only light up Arab writing but writing as a whole.

# Vision and Image
## The Naked Eye and the Eye of the Heart

### 1

In a saying attributed to Ibn Sukkara, the poet describes poetry as: 'A form of speech, which if it wishes, can enchant and transmute images. It is not afraid to go against the consensus nor constrain the natural disposition.'[1] What applies to poetry applies to art in general. However, art as enchantment and transmuter of images, raises questions about the significance of image in art and about the significance of seeing.

### 2

I am inclined to say that there is a metaphysical, religious dimension to the issue of image and figuration in Islam; the question is not confined to the canon of religious law, as some people maintain, nor is it something that has a narrow religious explanation, as others say.

Idolatry expresses itself through figuration, for the most part in sculpture or paintings. Belief in the singularity of God not only represents the abandonment of idolatry but also a disclosure of the essence of existence, its bare substance. The principal and fundamental expression of this disclosure is abstract and based on the alphabet. The alphabet is abstract, or calligraphic – a drawing, which doesn't refer to 'the real world' but rather to 'the invisible world'.

The alphabet, in this sense, allows for the creation of a sphere, in which divine abstraction conforms to the expressive abstraction of words, and linguistic signs conform to divine signs. That is because God is a word, not an image. God is not known through image because such an image would present a false visual perception of him; he is only known through the words of the mind or the heart, which are abstract.

It has been said that God is also 'a creator'. In that case, why is man not able to use 'pictorial image' as much as 'the word' to express himself? The answer lies in the fact that pictorial images are sensual. They will bind man to something sensory and material, which will lead him astray and distance him from the non-sensual nature of God. The word 'non-representational' affirms the difference between Islam and idolatry and the divergence of the one from the other. It is clear therefore that the singularity of God ordains that expression should abandon idolatry and idolatrous forms, which are approximations of the divinity. It enjoins the spiritual, i.e. that meaning should be abstract, internal, something beyond the object/ the image, not something in it. The expression in words should be accomplished in such a manner that the words themselves are freed from nature or material concerns, as happens vocally in music or through the craft of calligraphy. Perhaps all of this explains the Arab-Islamic form of adornment, known as arabesque. It is a drawing in which the line appears to be a word or melody. It is a form of calligraphic music, or an utterance, of which only the essence can be expressed, since it appears to have no subject or external source.

The self contemplates the image from outside, but such a

distinction does not exist in a word. The impression that the image generates is primarily sensual, while the impression that the word generates is abstract and originates in the mind, the soul or the heart – it comes from the innermost reaches of being. The image is a reflection in one form or another, of a reality that has a prior existence. It is an 'imitation', in one form or another. The word is the naming of a thing and the creation of reality: 'Be and it is.' Therefore divine image is not image but it is the bringing into being – i.e. it is the creative word 'Be'. The image, in addition, can turn what is being represented into an idol, i.e. into a 'god' that is respected, venerated and sanctified, and worshipped in the place of God, the one, the only. This means that no thing, or to be exact no human being, should be represented pictorially because there is a greater danger that such an image could transform him into an idol/a god than the danger posed by the image of a material object.

This might shed light on the phenomenon of the *hijab* in Islamic-Arab society. The veil conforms logically and naturally with a strictly monotheistic abstract view, which rejects the sensual and what stimulates it. In this case, the veil, which covers a woman's face, is merely a means of effacing her image – the source of temptation. In other words, it is only a confirmation of the fundamental truth of the spiritually abstract and the abandonment of the world of sensory perception and instincts.

In the light of the above, we can understand the significance that is accorded to words and linguistic signs, by which I mean rhetoric (*bayan*), in Islam. Rhetoric is not a substitute for image but it is the most flawless way of expressing meaning or truth. Through it the meaning of beauty and the aesthetic values of Islam are revealed. What is beautiful in Islam is what cannot be represented. It is what escapes the sensual and what transcends sensory perception. Beauty is lofty and supreme; it cannot be contained in a sensory form, nor can it be evaluated by the senses. Artistically, this means that aesthetic value is not contained in the 'image' or 'form' but in its meaning, and that beauty can be found only in infinity, which cannot be represented or in what cannot be 'given form'. Strictly speaking, this means that beauty is what canonical law determines is beautiful.

## 3

We know that the term 'moulder/creator' is one of the great names of God, and it is he who has fashioned all existing things and has given them their diversity and multiplicity, a particular form, a shape, which distinguishes them from the rest.

Every object is the visible-apparent image of itself and the ideative, concealed image. The image of an object is not restricted, as some people think, to its outward appearance but comprises its innate sense, i.e. its truth and meaning as well. Thus we see that those who are content to copy the external appearance of an object (representing it as a reality – as it appears to the eye) present only a superficial part of it, in addition to which it is a valueless reproduction. When we represent the superficial appearance of an object, we have a false image of it; in order to get a real sense of it, we must conceive it, that is, we must explain its sense and its meaning and we must represent it for that reason in accordance with that conception.

To put it another way, we should represent objects according to how we know them or see them with 'the eye of the heart', as the Sufis say. Image in the true sense of the word does not mean copying so much as clear expression of meaning and sense: the image of another creation.

## 4

I said: if we represent an object, it means first of all that we must conceive it. Herein lies the meaning of vision. For we do not see things properly when we content ourselves with looking at their exterior. We do not conceive or contemplate the world and its objects in their entirety when we content ourselves with reproducing their external appearance. If we intend to represent what we see physically, then the image will be limited to the external appearance of what we see, and this external appearance that we see is not everything that we see and neither is it the truth of what we see.

In fact, representing the external appearance will not lead to a complete equivalence between the object and its image. For however much we imitate the external appearance of the flower, we cannot produce a flower – only an exact image of it.

The artist has a right to use natural objects and living beings as models for his work. But we also have the right to ask what he means by his imitation. Is it merely a copy? Is he playing at seeing how the model he is copying appears in paint or sculpture? Or is he trying to compete with nature?

In the first two instances, the artist has to recognize that he is not using the human characteristic that has been given to him and that sets him apart from other creatures and makes him essentially distinct. For what sets man apart from other creatures is his capacity to create, not his capacity to copy. Copying is a work of repetition, which neither enriches the capacity to create nor makes it more profound. On the contrary, it trivializes and impoverishes it, as it trivializes and impoverishes the world. He must also recognize, if he harbours a desire to compete with nature, that however distinguished a copyist he might be, his work will always be less beautiful and less subtle than the thing he is copying.

A copy remains a sign that man is refusing to use the creative power that marks him out. Or perhaps it conceals a tendency to cover up the fragmentation and inconsistencies in the world or a hatred and rejection of the self.

5

Conformity or similarity is not a creative condition. What is the point of painting the exterior of an apple, for example, down to the smallest possible detail, as Matisse once asked? What is the use of transcribing something that nature already presents in vast quantities?

Indeed, the more realistic a copy of reality is, the further away it is from reality.

The likeness is illusory. The likeness is an expression of a non-artistic nature.

'I imitated him' or 'I copied' him means 'I acted' or 'I spoke like him', equally, I did not disregard him. Imitation is not done with the purpose of producing a beautiful act or saying but, on the contrary, with the purpose of producing something ugly. Imitation is intrinsically ugly and only generates ugliness – in the lowest form of 'art'. The Prophet Muhammad is reported to have said, 'Imitating someone [i.e. by performing his deeds or speaking his words] has never made me happy. If imitating the deeds and speech of man is ugly, imitating things is even worse.'[2]

Mankind, because he is a rational being, is by nature creative. He does not ape or imitate man or nature (things) but only looks at everything as a creative rational being, i.e. as an originator, an innovator.

6

If we give expression to some thing or other, by giving it form – if we represent it – then we are presenting an image that is different from its specific external image: in other words we are 'overturning' its image.

Artistically speaking, the sensory perception of a thing does not develop until a distance has developed between the thing and its direct external reality. In this sense, strictly speaking, art cannot be realistic. In fact, the word 'reality' appears contradictory and foolish – since art emerges only where there is no sign of similarity. It is smoke without fire. It is true that it is possible to copy the external appearance in a technical or scientific way, but this copy is not art, merely a craft or a science.

Let us take an example. The chair that the artist draws has been drawn before. A craftsman, a carpenter, drew it (represented it). The craftsman imitated (represented) the 'concept' of the chair, and the chair was limited by this 'concept'. (It is a chair that is limited by this concept.) Therefore there is the 'concept' of the chair, then the 'real' chair (the crafted/the represented) and then the 'artistic' chair (the copy).[3] The artist here is imitating a work that was originally based on an imitation. The drawing here (the image) is third-rate (the lowest of the low) in relation to the true nature (the highest) of things.

According to this theory of art, nature is not something that should be imitated, copied and replicated, but, on the contrary, something that should be contemplated, reflected upon and discovered. Artistic language is not given to creators so that they can reproduce the world and imprison its known, external images, but so that they can free it, maintaining its internal dynamism, for infinity, and making it appear continually in new images.[4]

7

Artistically, the world is an illusion.

Artistically, the world does not exist in the world, but rather in what lies behind it. It is necessarily somewhat abstract, as if the image-maker is conceiving an image that will wipe out the image. In wiping it out, he creates a presence – a transparent weaving – which does not refer to direct reality, rather to its meaning and its sense. As meaning and sense are unlimited, it refers to their infinity.

8

Arab calligraphy and adornment represent a perfect example of this sense of infinity. They neither represent nor imitate. Ibn Abbas has described calligraphy as a prayer spoken by the hand's tongue. They eradicate all forms of image in order to evince the infinity of meaning (truth). This demonstrates the supreme importance of beauty and the sense of beauty. A saying attributed to Imam Ali is, 'Beautiful calligraphy makes the truth clearer.' It is just as possible to say: 'Beauty enhances the truth clearly.'

9

The word *kalima* is feminine, pregnant with primitive, creative powers. It constantly places us in a never-ending horizon. This is what it enjoins when it is transformed into a line. When the letter is transformed calligraphically it enters a geographical infinity: it bends and undulates, intertwines with itself and meets itself face to face, becomes circular and elongates, clothes movement in all its dimensions and stores up all the signs. From this perspective, the creator, whether he is working with words, calligraphy or colour, is interested only in what he sees insofar as it is a step to what he does not see. It is as if the image is a curtain that we have to penetrate to see the truth that lies behind it. Given that the universe is constantly changing, its appearance is constantly ceasing. It is not the task of the creator to represent this 'ceasing', to mask and paint it, in order to fix it, for in so doing he will do no more than make clear what does not need to be made clear. On the contrary, his task is to establish lines and forms between him and this 'vanishing', which allow him to see the profound dynamic behind it. His task is to bring the viewer face to face with this infinity, through its forms and its rhythms: to confront him with an unknown distance, which, however near it becomes, will always remain distant and unknown.

The line in its primordial sense is like the word, what precedes formation, i.e. what comes before reality: it is absent or concealed, or what lies behind the overt, in relation to the realistic apparent.

Every thing that is created in word or in calligraphy is not concerned with what is seen unless it is as a step to what is not seen. It is concerned only with image – ornamentally or formally, to the extent that it conceals the sense and points to a meaning. The significance of the image does not lie in its visible surface but rather in the fact that it is a threshold to whatever meaning it has and a door that leads the spectator to what is behind it: the absent or the abstract, in its essence or nature. To put it another way, the significance of the image is contained not in its visual appearance but in what it indicates or symbolizes. The image is like a curtain that we must pierce in order to see what lies behind – what deserves to be seen or recalled.

Line is a symbol and another form of words – letters, which are also symbols as well. It is limitlessly able to create form, as a 'sensual-realistic and imaginary' extension at the same time. Thus the lines harmoniously form what look like mirrors, which reflect the unseen aspects of the visible world. Thus the world appears, through the harmonious arrangement of the lines and the words, to be a system of signs. Man himself is a symbol and a sign. Everything is a symbol and a sign. Things and beings are all lines – symbols on this page – which we call the world or reality or existence.

Because the universe is constantly evolving, so its manifestation is constantly ceasing. It is not the task of the creator to 'represent' this 'ceasing', to place masks and colours in images, in order to 'fix' them, since in doing that he does no more than 'clarify' what is already clear – explain what does not need to be explained. Indeed, his task, on the contrary, is to establish lines and form between himself and this 'ceasing', which allow him to see the profound dynamic behind it: he tries to understand the truth of the world and remain in contact with its mysteries and its dimensions. His task is, through his forms and rhythms, to place the spectator constantly face to face with infinity.

# 10

It is not as easy to see things as people believe. They are obfuscated by previous readings and 'images', filled with ready-made premises and accumulated usages. It is a struggle to free the word from these prior associations in order to be able to see it as if for the first time. We must read things (look at them) with the innocent eyes of a child, so that we can write them or represent them in their original pure state.

# 11

This takes us on to what I shall call the 'mysticism' of art. We should not confuse the word here with the burden of its religious-historical associations, but regard it only as an embodiment of an artistic vision. I will lay out the following points, by way of explanation.

1. 'Mysticism' here does not mean detaching oneself from the real world, but only detaching oneself from its overt appearance, in order to attain its depths and plunge into its inner dimension, that which goes beyond the apparent to the concealed and from the 'present' to the 'absent'.

2. The expression here points to the living experience, not to speculative abstraction. Mysticism transcends rationalism and its system of thought and goes beyond it to life and intuition. In other words, if philosophy judges intuition and experience, using reason and logic, Sufism, by contrast, judges reason and logic through experience and intuition.

3. This mysticism does not reject life as ephemeral, as 'religious Sufism' does, but only rejects it as a 'veil' that cloaks true life. On the contrary it is as much concerned with life as with the body, but it does not stop at the apparent – rather, it struggles to reveal the other side of the world and things.

4. This 'mysticism' is not still or fixed in one place, but is constantly travelling through things to the heart of the world. Thus it looks at the world as an unending movement, and looks at creation as an infinite journey inside this movement.

5. It is a form of mysticism that unites dream and reality and, in that, it is a harmonization between contradictory parts. Night, for example, is no longer the opposite of day but becomes a completion of it or another face of it.

6. It is a form of mysticism that asserts that the profound meaning of man lies in his endless quest for the infinite; the character of this art is derived from how it expresses this infinity.

7. It is a form of mysticism that does not concern itself with common and general matters, which we know about, but with what we do not know about – the unknown. This means that it is the nature of the artistic vision always to reveal the 'child/infant' of the world.

8. It is a form of mysticism that is transformative since it is constantly acting to present the world in new and different images, through new and different experiences.

9. It is neither a closed form of mysticism nor 'captive' in any way (philosophically or religiously), but is open and dynamic.

10. Creativity in this form of mysticism is spontaneous. It is as the Sufi expressions themselves describe it, a dictation or flood or *shath,* uncontrolled by any form of logic. It is creativity that originates from a phase 'which goes beyond the rational phase'.

## 12

How far these expressions are from 'the mechanistic culture'!

If it is correct to call our age 'the mechanistic age', then such sayings appear to come from another age. Here aesthetic creativity allows us to redefine the meaning of 'progress' and the meaning of 'age' but this is another matter.

Machinery, essentially, is functional – beneficial.

Aesthetic creativity comes from nature, not from machinery. Machinery is concerned with things as things, and creativity is concerned with the link between man and things. It is the link that is embodied in a language, which does not only convey dreams but is itself a dream.

There is no mechanical intermediary between the hand and the paper on which it is drawing or writing or the material that is painted or sculpted. The pen or the paintbrush is an extension of the hand, a part of it, another finger. Thus, the hand produces directly. What results from technology is indirect for it lacks the touch of excitement.

The hand subjects matter to a sensual-affective interplay (of senses – excitement). Technology is detached. It separates man from matter for it destroys the emotional relationship between them.

## 13

Abstraction frees art from the functional weight of media or belief. Only art, which has been liberated from this functionalism, is able to realize pure excitement.

Functionality or usefulness is linked to the primitive, and in the past the primitive was a gauge for assessing art. Now we perceive the external world objectively and are able to distinguish between the useful and the beautiful and therefore are able to enjoy something for itself and detached from its uses. We enjoy the poem or the painting or the sculpture as a work of 'beauty', not as something 'useful'.

Primitivism looks only at the use of something, the tree, for example. A tree that fruits is considered better than one that doesn't, although the latter might be more beautiful. We have not yet freed ourselves in our 'modern' society from the 'primitive' view.

When we insist that art be beneficial, we damage its original role, for which nothing can be substituted; we accord it a role that can be better realized through the different forms of media. In other words, we kill art when we transform it into a tool – a form of technology.

If it is necessary to study art from the point of view of functionality, then its function is theoretical rather than 'practical'. It is ideative-effective, like prayer. It is a 'link' between man and the world of reflection at the high and low tides of existence, in man and his fate, in the mysteries of the universe. It kindles the emotion and imagination in man to practise this meditation.

## 14

The classical Greeks copied the 'body' of nature, while those who preceded them (the Sumerians, the Babylonians, the Phoenicians) attempted to draw their thoughts about the thing; because of that they did not concern themselves with the details of what they were imitating but only with the expression of it.

Artists in Islam replace imitation with the creation of 'artistic things', as opposed to things in reality. Those before them try to 'depict' the world, in one form or another, whereas the Muslim artist tries to construct another world inside this world. The primary interest of the former is the thing, but the primary interest of the Muslim is to create because the thing represents a link and it did not have an existence on its own.

Before Islam the artist saw with the eye of the body, but in Islam the artist sees with the eye of the heart.

The first perceives the world as an existence – perched in front of him, which has material weight. The second perceives the world as postponed or suspended. The 'perspective' of the first permits a constant visual repetition of the thing, transferred from one place to another: what is seen in nature can be reproduced on paper, wood or stone. The 'perspective' of the second, by contrast, allows the person to see something other behind it. The first is concerned with the objectivity of existence while the second is concerned with its essence.

## 15

It is the 'eye of the heart' that draws and the body is no more than a 'witness'. Since the artist looks at the world with 'the eye of the heart', he transforms it into something that cannot be contained or formed in an image, into a 'thing/non-thing' or a form/non-form. Through his work, he tries to 'overturn' the world, in order to take it close to the mysterious and the invisible. It is as if his physical task lies in bringing the invisible out of the visible and the transparent out of the dense. It is correct to see that we can see only what is visible in the dense, but it is also true to say that we can see in the transparent only what we are unable to see with the eyes of the body.

This sight frees the seer and what is seen. Thus it is possible to say that, artistically, the thing is constantly being reborn even at the time of its death. In fact, the moment it dies is the moment it is born.

## 16

Artistic creativity is a question that not only concerns the world but that also should be put to art itself. When we speak about plastic arts in Arab creation, we should be constantly asking and reasking questions about the meaning of seeing and the meaning of image.

# Creativity and Form

1

The question of form from the perspective of creativity brings us face to face with poetic creativity in our past. We all know that poetry in Arab society developed socially, i.e. the form it has assumed is the product of a social experience. This might explain the wish and desire of society to preserve the ancient poetical form, even though the poet has adopted new content. It is sufficient to glance at the current controversy over tradition versus innovation and modernity to see that this issue has assumed the importance of a great national problem. Thus it seems as if the Arabs regard these forms as a national expression of their identity in the context of what they say about themselves and life and the universe, or, to put it another way, they regard them as having an intrinsic value that is almost sacred. It is not surprising that the abandonment of such forms is tantamount to an abandonment of their identity. People with such attitudes perceive the ancient form of the Arab *qasida* (ode) as being inextricably bound up with Arab history, culture and national identity. Consequently, they believe that any form of modification will constitute a change in Arab cultural principles and Arab poetic identity. When people with such attitudes respond to calls for a renewal of the forms or changes to them, they maintain that any innovations in poetry should be limited to ideas and subjects, and say that the ancient poetic form is able to embrace and express any new ideas, however novel they are. This school of thought holds that any developments in the field of culture and art must conform to Arab artistic and cultural principles and must follow them exactly, in the same way as anything that develops in the field of religion must submit to the standards of religious principles – the area of morals, legislation and the supernatural.

In the Arab world, there is objective support for this stance. For forms, which are the product of social experience, as is the case with the Arab poetic form, will not change unless there is a change in the socio-cultural experience that produced them and a change in the values that sprang from this experience, the mindset of society and the way it relates to things and views the world. It is difficult today to say that Arab society has departed radically from this experience. On the contrary, as a whole, it has not yet moved on from the rhetoric and memory of the oral tradition and practice to the age of writing and technology. This means that conditions in Arab society have not developed sufficiently to allow the ancient function of poetic forms to change. Indeed, the development or alteration of a form demands the appearance of a new function, which will emerge only from a society that has changed its traditional structure and the way it relates to things. Therefore, it enjoins the freedom of the individual and the right of free speech and thought. This is not available in Arab society. For the concept of the individual as a being who is free to believe in what he wants and say what he wants does not exist and is not acceptable, even on a theoretical and speculative level. This concept continues to be rejected today by the 'regime' and the 'party' as it has already been rejected by the *umma* (community of Islam).

I would add that, because of permanent elements and the conjunction between 'the political', 'the religious' and 'the linguistic', the forms of poetry in Arab society have assumed a religious or quasi-magical function: a function of identity in the first instance, as I have pointed out. These forms are tied at one and the same time to the individual and the social unconscious. In the Arabic language, no poetry exists outside these forms: this is what the establishment and the *umma* have decreed. It is as if these forms have been revealed from on high, from the musical sky, in a single and eternal expression, which is in complete conformity with the Arab identity and character.

This brings us to the three principles that are the basis for the view of poetry adopted by the dominant cultural order.

1. The poetic form in Arab poetry is basically a musical mould: the rhythmical beats are arranged in a particular sequence, which is called metre (*bahr*).

2. This systematic arrangement has a metaphysical (ontological) sense: the essence, which orally addresses the world directly, is the musical-metrical essence.

3. Poetic metres have an objective-material existence, which reaches beyond the desires of individuals, since they have a social value and a civilizing-cultural basis.

2

Perhaps the above goes some way to explain the lack of interest in Arab poetic criticism in form. It is evident that not only critics but also readers fail to concern themselves with it. For the most part they are interested in the content, which is a direct result of the predominance of a culture with a particular ideological make-up in Arab society. In fact, if someone shows himself to be even slightly concerned with the form of a poem, he is accused of being a 'form-monger' – his work is ridiculed and he is shunned. According to this school of thought, the principles measure not only the poetical nature of the poetry but also the nationalism of the poet and his membership of the Arab race. His poetry is judged according to the extent to which it adheres to these principles. On the whole, it is a random ideological judgment, which is based on a kind of associative bigotry, guided by politics and for the most part by an ignorance of these very principles. The irony here is that what gives these principles their splendour and strength is the form. The form in poetry from the Jahiliyya period, not the content, is the distinguishing feature of its creative presence. The Qur'an itself is primarily a form, since it establishes a way of expression that was unknown before and it is this way of expression that, strictly speaking, distinguishes it from speech. If this standpoint in relation to poetry, in the strict sense of the word, is sound and coherent, it will not be confirmed by the copying of these principles, but rather by their emulation – i.e. the creation of new forms of expression, confirming the creativity of the Arab people and the vitality and continuous renewal of Arab thought.

Forms are images. Inasmuch as images are many and varied, they reveal the riches and the diversity of vision and seeing and the riches of the world that they are revealing. Inasmuch as images are scarce and constrained in restrictive moulds and external form, it is an indication of their impoverishment and the poverty of the world that they are revealing.

I do not doubt that there is a wealth of talent in Arab writing today. Nevertheless, it seems to me that the literary world is narrow and limited. This goes back fundamentally to the fact that this talent is controlled by a traditional culture, which tends to make the world narrow by confining it in a traditional straitjacket and preventing the evolution of ideas that go beyond its limits, sometimes in the name of religion and at other times in the name of politics or identity.

This helps to explain why, in this traditional culture, there is a force that compels Arabs to criticize any variation or change in form, as I have pointed out, and makes them imagine that by adhering to such forms they are helping to maintain the traditions and stabilizing their sense of identity. Some of them regard such changes as an indication of changes in the writer himself – i.e. a corruption of his identity and consequently a corruption of his work. Therefore some poets are accused of treason, of being agents or Zionists for doing nothing more than writing in ways that do not conform to tradition. This understanding of identity, which rests on singularity and unity, is a simplification, which flattens the world and empties it of meaning and disfigures the humanity of mankind.

## 3

This view of form dominates the Arab cultural establishment and Arab taste in general. Nevertheless, for one reason or another, it should be studied separately. There has been a change concerning individual creativity, a change in its relationship to things – the things of the real and the transcendental worlds – and a change in its relationship with values and the existing measures based on traditions – Bedouin and religious in particular. The poetic concern starts to focus on how to reveal unknown beauty instead of focusing on describing known beauty. The value of a subjectivist as distinct from a collectivist approach begins to be discovered. It uncovers in particular its freedom and independence and its individual desires. The poet starts to benefit from different forms of culture, especially contemplative philosophy and the Sufi experience, as well as art and architecture in particular. This allows imagination and imaginative elements to be more receptive and gives both mind and body more freedom and presence. Language has to find an answer to all of this, and the poet begins to use figurative language in particular, to the extent that it become an internal wave in the lake, which we call the *qasida*.

From an architectural standpoint, the structure of the poetic sentence becomes a form of musical-geometry. It is a structure that basically depends on a knowledge of combinations between sound-letters and silent-letters, between words and between sentences.

This knowledge is what enables the poet to make his poem a vast space, which is undulating and still at the same time.

It appears, when viewed from this angle, that the geometrical dimension is one of the dimensions that make up the poetic form. It is a dimension that is represented in the elements, which make the form a coherent structure, free from any brittleness, gratuitousness or unnecessary tricks. Because of this dimension, it is possible for the *qasida* to be a building with arches, windows and domes. Or to be a city with streets, arcades and bridges. We can see the movement of shadow and light. We see corners and curves and steps. We can see breadth and depth and height.

This is what paved the way for the form of the modern *qasida* to become a symphony of movement and light, depth and surface, calligraphy and drawing, emptiness and repletion, visibility and invisibility. It has enabled the form to become an image, which signifies the sense – the meaning, both of which lie behind the formation, a power, which is endlessly receptive. To put it another way, it is what led to the almost entire elimination of the Khalili metrical moulds[1] and to the focusing of poetic writing around kinetic power. It is a power that indicates that the invisible part of the *qasida* form is richer and more important than its visible sense, since the form is no longer a mould but has become an indication of the internal fire, the fire of the experience of writing.

The form is no longer a mould: this phrase denotes a complete upheaval in the way poetry and form are understood. It is no longer possible to speak of a form (or a metre or poetic measure) as having a previous and ready-made existence, which is independent of the essence of the poem. In poetry, the form has become something that is defined by the way the poetic work is defined. And since poetry is infinite, its forms are infinite. This is all represented in what I call the elimination of a standard authority.

It is useful in this context to point out that the form in Arab architecture has experienced a much richer and more varied development than poetry, and that can be attributed, I believe, to the fact that there has been no standard authority in architecture as has been the case in poetry.

This is analogous with the Sufi experience of religious jurisprudence, religious law and philosophy. The Sufis transformed religion into a personal experience and went beyond religious law and the literal meaning of the Qur'an to what they called truth (God) and the inner world, and replaced the rationalist methodology of knowledge with another form of knowledge. The Sufi experience completely overturned the existing concept of knowledge in establishing new ways of relating to the universe and God and to man and to language.

Thus everything that is connected to architecture and Sufism is a creative and dynamic factor. So the prohibition of any form of physical representation in religion has allowed the imagination to invent new abstract means of expression. With the abandonment of nature, new broad fields are opened up for the work of impression, knowledgeable play and imagining. The rejection of the apparent, material world makes it possible to plunge into what lies behind it, the concealed inner world. During the Jahiliyya period and in the first years of Islam, the profound meaning of poetry lay in its expression of the visible known; now, by contrast, it lies in its expression of the invisible, what cannot be seen with the naked eye, the intangible. Writing poetry from this perspective means putting into images what cannot be put into images. The aim is no longer to represent the realistic appearance, but the internal essence instead.

In this way, the concept of form changes as well. The form of the *qasida* begins to go further than the illustrated appearance of the words to what comprises its inner meaning. In addition to being dimensions and associations made up of words and commas, points, blanks and visible lines, the form becomes a series of unseen dimensions and associations, which are the product of countless forms of figurative language (fantasy, image, allegory, etc). We should add that this change reveals a dimension of time in the form as well as one of movement, which is generated by the meeting between place and time – a meeting that the musicality/rhythm instigates and brings alive.

Thus the Arab poet has reestablished his links with the cultures that preceded Islam, those of Sumeria, Babylon, Greece, Persia and

India, through the deep-rootedness of this culture in poetry and thought, painting and dramatic representation, architecture and music.

4

The apparent and the concealed or, let us say, the visible and the invisible are terms that are key to the understanding of modern poetic experience and what shapes it. In this experience, which is basically Sufi, every thing and every phenomenon has two characteristics, which are concealed and apparent: a prime example of how two characteristics are united in one thing and one phenomenon is the human body. We experience the inner concealed nature of the body (its identity, imagination, emotions and senses), on the one hand, and the apparent manifest nature on the other (we can see and touch it like any other object).

Therefore, in understanding this experience, we must initially distinguish between the concealed and the apparent in every thing and in every phenomenon.

We should initially point to the fact that the manifest nature of an object is not only its external appearance, but is also the form in which the thing is revealed, or it is its shape and image. In other words, this revelation is the visibility of this object or its visible side, and the manifestations of objects are what we call the world or existence.

And if its apparent nature is one way of revealing the object, then its inner nature is another way of revealing it.

The basic question, in terms of knowledge, is how to know or how to be aware of these inner natures.

In this poetic experience, which is Sufi at source, as I have pointed out, existence is therefore something that is seen and unseen at the same time. It is apparent and hidden, and what can be seen of it is only an indication of what cannot be seen.

The visible side is limited, finite. The invisible side is unlimited and infinite.

Most people, whether they are artists or not, live in the visible world and are content with it. The visible, the bright, that which is perceptible through the senses: this is what the Greek aesthetic view is based upon.

The invisible, the concealed, the obscure: this is what the Arab Sufi aesthetic is based upon, and continues the ancient aesthetic of the Babylonians and the Sumerians and, to a certain extent, the Muslims – in the limits of the Qur'anic text. The Hellenistic aesthetic view has led to poetry (and art in general) imitating the visible side of things, to a greater or lesser extent, in one form or another, or to the imitation (mimesis) of a model or an object that has a prior existence. The value of the artistic work lies in the fineness of the imitation and its detail.

The second view works to disclose and express the invisible inner nature of objects, in one form or another. By rejecting the representation of visible things and imitating or copying them, this opens up a new world to the visionary and the visionary artist and to writing and to the art of writing.

5

How do we see the invisible? Or what tools do we use to see it?

With neither the senses nor reason, answers poetic experience. We can see it only with what we call the eye of the heart, or intuition or illumination, that is, by other forms of gnostic revelation, which can be applied to the invisible inner nature. Only by 'obliterating' the exterior (sense, reason) will the visionary be in a fit state to 'fix' its inner nature or be able to bring together the inner world of the visionary (the knower) and the inner world of what is seen (the object of the knowledge).

Knowledge is not seeing the visible; knowledge is seeing what lies behind it: the invisible. It is knowing the internal nature of objects.

What we perceive with our senses, in particular what we call reality, is a being that has no fixed nature. It lives in constant motion, disintegrating and disappearing. In order to obtain a true and knowledgeable sight of it, we must penetrate it to see what lies behind it, going deep into its nucleus, from where the motion of life spurts forth and which contains its creative abilities. Thus reality is no more than revelations and representations of this nucleus. Everything is the nucleus of a coming together of numerous appearances and forms. The object according to the Sufi poetic vision is capable of being all representations. There is no end to its representations. The representation/the revelation does not exist outside this nucleus.

Thus, in writing, in expression, the poet attempts to sink down (or to rise to) the nucleus of objects and to put this attempt into language in a form/representation.

This attempt only achieves an all-engulfing agitation, which shakes the body until delirium-trance occurs. Thus, the poet does not express the meaning of things (its nucleus, its infinity) so much as his own experience: the agitation of delirium, captivation by meaning and infinity; he does not express meaning because it is not fixed but is in perpetual motion through birth and renewal.

Writing, as far as he is concerned, is, in this way, one of the forms of metaphysical knowledge. It is a form that transcends the perceptible appearance of things, to their internal dimension, to their essence.

Gnostic knowledge, unlike rational-scientific knowledge, penetrates the mystery of the phenomenon, the inner nature of the object. As I have pointed out, it uses intuition-illumination, delirium-trance. What is contained in art or poetry is different from this sense of intoxication. Poetry and art, in general, convey agitation – delirium – but do not convey the idea or the subject.

Thus, it is possible to see why, in the Sufi experience, neither poetry nor art can be imitative. For imitating a model of which you have prior knowledge is at odds with this sense of delirium. Strictly speaking, art in the general sense of the word is not an expression of things but of the delirium of the body – of life in the way in which they fuse with the meaning of the world and its mysteries, though things. Art is like life: birth and death in this delirium. Rather, the insignificance of death is itself life in this delirium.

The poet or the artist, according to this experience, does not start from something that has gone before, be it object or idea, but himself creates thoughts and facts, from the changes through which he has lived on this journey – the journey of delirium – which will take him to the endless path of meaning.

6

The word itself, according to this poetic experience, keeps on renewing its meaning and has no prior or ready-made meaning, as is the case in common language. In the language of prose, everyday conversation and transaction, the word is merely equivalent to a vessel, which carries something. For basically, it is functional and useful. Therefore it is not adopted for itself but rather for its practical function. It is nothing more than a tool or a means to something.

However, in the poetic experience, it takes on an another dimension.

Let us say that the word is a visible/apparent element, although its sense is concealed. It takes on this sense only after it has been stripped of its previous meanings, paths and context. It is stripped bare of everything except its letters and musicality. This divestment is what prepares it to enter the context of inner meaning.

Once it is stripped bare of former external covering, it can open up to countless relationships and forms. To put it another way, it becomes a receptacle for expressive possibilities, which are in harmony with its inner world and possibilities.

Thus every piece of text has two levels of meaning: the visible, apparent sense and the invisible, inner sense. The words on their own do not make up the text or give it its identity but rather they are the ideative-affective charge. It is this charge that is particularly important when studying a text, while aestheticism, which is based on what is known, is repetition, so the creator sees its special essence, in content and form, in the inner sense (the invisible, the unknown). Because of that the elements that go into its formation or writing are not external and prepared (metre, pun), but, rather, a dictation from the inner world. For the inner sense is what dictates the apparent, and saying that the apparent (the formula) must dictate the inner world kills the dynamic of creativity.

The form therefore is not the external ordering of prescribed elements, but rather a crystallization of the inner dynamic, or it is a visible thing through which and in which the inner world is revealed. As the appearance is the appearance of a specific inner world, so the form cannot be generalized or formulaic but a movement that follows the movement of the appearance. It is the appearance itself in the state of crystallization or in the state of forming.

Let us say: the form is a written link between the inner and the apparent worlds. Or it is a linguistic-calligraphic zone between the visible and the invisible.

As the profundity of the saying comes from its invisible nature, so the form of what is said is also invisible. The exterior and its forms are a ready-made achievement. But the form in the poetic experience, to which I am referring, does not come from the prepared – rather it comes from the inner world, which is never prepared and which remains capable of and open to being moulded. This shows how poetic sayings neither imitate daily life (reality) nor nature.

7

Poetic speech does not convey the appearance of nature or life for several reasons:

1. The language in which the creator names the things is itself a creative language. The poet, like the Sufi, imitates the creator: he says things as if he is creating them anew. Without this element, speech and language are imprisoned in an endless reiteration of the known and visible nature of things, which is a fruitless task.

2. Repeating the visible does not explain it; on the contrary, it confuses and veils it.

3. Language in poetic experience is existence – since it is the birthplace of creation and what gives it its name. Sufi writing is life and is not a mere expression of life. Life is the act of becoming and changing. Writing similarly is the act of becoming and changing.

4. Imagination is a faculty of inventing forms and images, a faculty of renewal, without which the dimension of the inner world could not be revealed. It is the light that takes the poet to the concealed worlds. It is what brings out his latent faculties. Because of this, it goes beyond the formulaic, the fixed in life and in writing, and sinks into the dynamic of experience through the force of imagination.

5. Thus when I say form, I mean creation. Creation as initiating act is necessarily manifest in the initiating form.

How can we give form to what cannot be given form, to the absolute? That is the question, and that is the challenge that faces the experience of poetic writing.

The issue is not about formula or appearance, but an issue of movement and the interior world.

8

If meaning is not visible, how can we put it, or how can we put the excitement of it into a visible representation or form?

The form 'house' is visible and belongs to an 'inhabitant' who is invisible. The form is a body – a body of meaning. Between the 'form' and 'meaning' is oneness, 'representation'.

The elements of form are everything that make up the body (the form) – the word, the way it relates to what come before and after it, its musicality and rhythm, the interspace, the blanks, the sentence and its structure, the image and imagination, the structure of the calligraphy or the simplified or constructional circles, etc.

Therefore it is possible to say that the most significant part of the form is the invisible – the representation. The invisible inner is what determines the visible exterior. This definition is what distinguishes the form of the said artistic work from any other form that has been achieved. It is not possible for one form to be similar to another, since such a similarity would indicate that the artistic work were merely a form with no inner life – not the product of an experience, but the product of a craft.

The essential component in any artistic work is its interior nature; it is this that dictates its exterior, in a matter commensurate with its own rules, not a set of objective-external rules or formulae.

The form is always unique. It is a different addition to the objective exterior and its visible objects. It is an emanation of the interior: to be exact, a specific appearance, which gives expression to a specific inner world and which is linked to it in substance. It does not refer us to a specific exterior, whether it is model or formula, but refers us to its essence.

In traditional terms, the inner world was something on which the external world imposed its conditions: the spontaneous delirium of the poet, as though it was extemporaneous, had to enter a ready-made mould, as though it were chained. The 'soul' found itself in a body that was prepared and shaped by external rules.

But in poetic experience, the apparent must submit to the concealed. The form accordingly is nothing more than a departure from the external, from the prepared and from the formalized and the formal. Its fundamentalism, vitality and meaning spring from its invisible nature, in particular, and from its requirements. In this you can find its newness and artistry.

9

'Creation and form': this is the title of the chapter. However it is clear, from what I have presented, that this title is erroneous, because it gives the impression that the artistic form has an independent existence. In art, and in poetry in particular, it is impossible to talk about form as an independent or absolute entity. The form, in poetry, and I am repeating myself here, is the clearly defined representation of a clearly defined artistic work. It changes according to the artistic work. It is the body of the artistic work. As one body is different from another, so one work of art is necessarily different from another. The form is not based on a previous formula or a set standard. It is a multiplicity, not a oneness: it is not based on a model, and it is not restrained in any way.

Therefore the title should read 'Creation/form.'

10

The entry for *shakl* (form) in the *Lisan al-Arab* dictionary is as follows:

1. *Shakl*: similarity and likeness (but similar to what? and like what?). The meaning of *ash-shakl* here demands a prior model. It indicates that *ash-shakl* is not original but is the ensuing result. It is a form of imitation. Lisan al-Arab says: this is similar to this, i.e. this is like this. And it says: someone is like someone, i.e. like him in his habits.

2. *Shakl*: manner followed, aim.

3. *Shaklu ash-shai'*: the perceptual image of an object or the imagined (what is invisible in the form). If we change the vowel and say *ash-shikl*, the word means coquetry of a woman,

flirtatiousness and flattery (is there something in this that reveals the aesthetic dimension in form?).

4. *Shakkala*: he fashioned something.

5. *ashkala/ashkula 'alaihi ash-shai'*: the seer saw it differently from what he thought, so he was dubious about it. *Al-mushkil* is derived from it and means a dubious matter.

6. *shakala al kitaba*: provided a piece of writing with vowel points; enchained it with desinential inflections, as if he removed from it doubts and dubiety. *Shaklu ash shai'* is its limitation and definition.

Thus *Lisan al-Arab* confirms that *shakl ash-shai'* means the image of something, enchaining it, defining it, and that changing the forms leads to problems.

Perhaps the above demonstrates how modern Arab poetry appears dubious and difficult to a great number of Arab readers. They believe, therefore, that the forms of poetry that they know (its metres) must remain unchanged because, without them, poetry loses its identity, and in the same way they believe the profound truths that it expresses about Arab identity will disappear: the poetry itself. For at a certain level, the death of such poetry is equivalent to the death of the Arabs.

There is a creative, civilized division: poetry can either be a creative force that is constantly being regenerated, i.e. given a new form, or it is nothing more than a series of moulds and rigid shapes. It can be ambiguous or it can be mere didactic and naïve rhetoric.

This division confirms that Arabs today, I mean the Arabs belonging to the prevailing cultural order, are attempting to live in a culture that has died, and are attempting to kill off the one culture that is alive.

# Rimbaud, Orientalist, Sufi

1

This article has a history.[1]

I became aware of Rimbaud's poetry at a time when I was involved with the study of Sufism, in particular its expressive-linguistic side. The more I read of his work, the more convinced I became that the Rimbaud of *L'Enfer* and *Illuminations* evinced the same sense of rapturous intoxication as Sufism did. I thought about translating his poetry into Arabic. The difficulties that I encountered and that forced me to postpone my work nevertheless provided me with a good opportunity to understand his experience.

I realized from the start that the cultural influences that have helped shape other Western writers and poets, by which I mean, on the one hand, the Greek tradition and, on the other, the Judaeo–Christian tradition, do not apply to Rimbaud's poetry; this means therefore that his experiences are unique, both in French culture itself and in French poetry.

Secondly, I realized that his letters to Izembard and Demeny demonstrate that he had become convinced of a new vision of the world and a new form of writing, which is based on Arab Sufi experience and writing: this is particularly evident in what he writes about the suspension of the senses in order to attain a state of translucency in the self, which will enable him to pierce through the solidity of the outer material world to its translucent inner self, where he will hear what cannot be heard and see what cannot be seen.

This is what spurred me on to read Rimbaud as an oriental Sufi poet.

## 2

Thus I read Rimbaud as an oriental-Sufi poet. By this, I mean that I find quintessential aspects of his poetry that are based on the Arab creative vision. The epithet 'Arab' here is ambiguous, so I will hasten to explain what I mean by it. I am using the word here in a particular sense and in a context in which race, nationalism and religion, strictly speaking, are set aside, so that the word signifies, instead, an exclusively cultural concept, whose roots extend to the era before Islam and the Arab language, to India and Persia and Greece, Sumeria and Babylon, across the prophecies of Judaism and Christianity. It is a concept whose various elements are more in tune with the Islamic climate, especially the Mediterranean, and whose identity is expressed in the Arabic language. I am reading Rimbaud as an Arab poet who is searching for an Arab dimension, in the broadest cultural sense, both in his poetic vision and in his experience.

The word 'orient' here refers to the Arab East, which forms an organic part of the orient as a whole; despite the diversity of its peoples, cultures and languages, it continues to represent a distinct unity *vis-à-vis* what we call the West.

3

Rimbaud was born, lived and died in the second half of the nineteenth century (20 October 1854 – 15 November 1891) and he spent more than ten years of his short life in an Arab-Islamic milieu. His first letter from Aden was dated 17 August 1880 and his last letter, also from Aden, was dated 30 April 1891. It was a century in which Europe witnessed decisive changes, brought about by new technology. It was also notable for its rejection of theological and feudal practices and the rise of imperial colonialism overseas. There was a return to Hellenistic rationalism, which contributed to the destruction of previously accepted ideas and mythical structures as a whole, and the establishment of the rational school.

While industrialism was the cornerstone of life in the West, Western thought analysed and criticized the self and the other at the same time. The concept of the other in Arab thought lay at the heart of its inquiries. Ernest Renan's stance on Ibn Rushd, which he presented in his dissertation on *Averroès et L'Averroïsme* on 11 August 1852, two years before Rimbaud was born, can be regarded as among the most brilliant of these critical inquiries into the Arab other. It is true that a critique of Arab thought based on Western ideas can be neither objective nor subtle, so it is possible to say that this critique demonstrated the development of Western thought rather than an understanding of the Arab other, Western rationalism. Nevertheless, it was the result of two basic streams of thought: Greek philosophy and Arab learning.

This rationalism was pivotal to a knowledge of matter. Since matter was resistant, it was necessary to struggle against it to discover its characteristics, in order to understand and transform it. The transformation of matter, as a thing or an object, led by necessity to the transformation of its essence. Thus Western rationalism began to express itself through constant research and enquiry into everything related to the object and the essence, or, to put it another way, into nature and culture. It is possible that Rimbaud believed, against the backdrop of these changes, that the Commune would be able to achieve some of the things for which it strived. But, as is well known, the Commune turned into a bloodbath and was immediately followed by the imposition of a moral order. The failure of the Commune had an unmistakable impact on Rimbaud's life and spirit, as he explained in his letter to Izembard. Perhaps *Une saison en enfer* is only a chapter about the political hell of France, i.e. a way of confronting that hellish reality, that semi-wildness.

4

In the climate of rationalism and technology, and in contrast to the overt rejection of the Arabic other, a movement grew up that was more receptive to Arab art and literature, and whose roots could be traced to the age of European enlightenment. There began to emerge a new form of awareness, which we might describe as an aesthetic awareness. It transcended the external and superficial view of the Arab East and its culture, i.e. the commercial and political perception, and also went beyond the merely descriptive, ornamental and decorative simplification. A widespread movement grew up that was inspired by the more profound creative dimension of the East, which was reflected in its poetry, stories and wisdom, its painting, stagecraft and music, which were well known among those specializing in the region. Translations of some of the greatest Arab Islamic works contributed to this movement. They included *The Thousand and One Nights* and works by Sufi authors, in particular, Farid al-Din al-Attar (*Kitab al-Nasa'ih*, or Book of Advice), which was translated by Silvestre de Sacy in 1819, and *Kitab Mantiq al-Tayr* (Conference of the Birds), which was translated by Garcin de Tassy in 1857 and published in 1864.

Thus at a time when rational-technical ideas reigned supreme, there began to emerge another stream of thought, which was more concerned with the esoteric aspects of the world, in particular those areas that escaped any attempt at rational definition. It manifested itself, for example, in research into the nature of infinity, magic and fantasy. The Western creator began to attach significance to relationships beyond the known and obvious causative connections that had a rational and empirical basis. I am referring here to relationships that result from other unknown forms of causality, which are not based on proven fact, relationships that generated endless mysterious feelings and which went beyond the bounds of reason and logic. This lay at the heart of the upheaval in Western writing, which resulted in the abandoning of Nicolas Boileau's (d. 1711) ideas on poetics, which were based on reason and had dominated poetic and literary ideas in general, and the substitution of another world of imagination, dream and the mysteries of magic in their place. When writing about *The Thousand and One Nights*, Borges refers to this as the extraordinary occupation of the West by the orient. This occupation ended rational influence over poetic, artistic and novel creativity as a whole and replaced it with a dimension of the infinite.

When we look at the huge Western creative output in poetry and painting and music and story-telling and drama, it appears as if the Western artist regarded the Arab East as a womb that had an endless supply of fantasies and forms. It is therefore not surprising that Goethe proclaimed in 1816, 'Save yourself. Go to the pure East and breathe in the breath of your fathers.' About fifty years later, Rimbaud said on fleeing from 'Western stagnation', 'I am going back to the East and to the first and eternal wisdom.'[2]

5

I don't intend to present academic precepts that will prove that Rimbaud was influenced by Arab Sufi thought. The issue of influence is not important in itself, since influence rests on historical and universal phenomena, which are closely associated with man's creative activities. Nothing in creative activity comes from nothing, and its essence is contained to a greater or lesser extent, in one form or another, in the presence of something else. Of more importance is the way in which creative activity is influenced, or the way in which creative essence uses the matter of influence and its components.

In this lecture, I shall also disregard what has been said about Rimbaud with regard to his knowledge of Arabic and the fact that he died a Muslim, and what has been said about Frederic Rimbaud, his father, who knew Arabic well, and translated the Qur'an into French as well as compiling a book on the Arab language. It is possible for a poet to know Arabic and be a Muslim and yet this still to mean nothing in the context of what we are going to look into in this research. However, we should point out that most Western researchers who have studied the impact of the orient on the West define the orient as being firstly Hellenistic and secondly Judaeo-Christian. In Rimbaud's poetry there is no significant trace of either Hellenistic or Judaeo-Christian culture, as I have pointed out, except in a negative sense, i.e. his poetry is almost completely devoid of these two cultures. The East in his poetry therefore represents something else.

In this article, I attempt to raise questions about this other thing, drawing attention to the fact that Rimbaud rebelled against Western culture and civilization in his use of elements that were not Western and which we can call Arabic, in the broad cultural meaning of the word, which I discussed at the beginning of the lecture, and that this led to the establishment in the French language of a poetic occident in oriental-Sufi thought.[3]

I am aware that, by so doing, this article on Rimbaud will raise many questions of a critical nature, especially as I have put on one side the vast number of critical studies about him, many of which contradict each other. Some critics, for example, regard him as an extreme revolutionary on the far left of the political spectrum, while others see him as a Christian, who underwent sin and salvation. Some see him as a precursor of Nietzsche, who proclaimed the idea of willpower and the *Übermensch* (superman), while for others he was someone who opposed religion and the icons of sex, nationalism and family. In this sense, he was surrealist. In this article, I will add another contradiction to these contradictions, which is more troubling because it completely removes Rimbaud from the context of Western critical tradition and places his poetry in another sphere altogether.

6

I shall begin by defining the external characteristics of Rimbaud's text, with particular reference to *Saison dans l'enfer* (Season in Hell) and *Les Illuminations* – these are the same characteristics as apply to Sufi text.

1. The first characteristic of this text is that it is closed (hermetic). It is unintelligible and obscure, and uses ancient conventions. The secret lies in the fact that the text is communicating an experience in the unknown, as is the case with Sufi writing, which is also communicating an invisible experience. It is a sublime experience despite being rooted in time, which it is impossible to frame and which goes beyond the limits of linguistic power. For words are limited in what they can say about a limitless experience. Language is derived from the world, while experience comes from what is beyond it; such experience is visionary and is constantly expanding. This is what al-Niffari is referring to, when he talks about the limitations of language: 'Each time the vision expands, the ways of expressing it shrink.'

   Therefore, language, which cannot properly convey the world of experience, is restricted in its ability to reveal another place to us, which is inexpressible and unutterable; when we wish to attain such a place, we can do so only by mystical means or what the Sufi called a state of ecstasy through which we can be connected to what is unspoken and indescribable.

This characteristic demonstrates that true poetry never explains and exposes but rather, on the contrary, pierces the obscure corners of the world. It is a form of perplexity, but a perplexity that is illuminated by intuition and the heart. To this extent, Rimbaud's text departed from Western culture norms, which were based on logical rationalism, i.e. on everything that conflicted with poetic knowledge, just as Sufi texts were based on the inner world, which was the subject of truth, and on the concealed – the unknown, which was the opposite of the manifest – the orthodox and what was established.

Just as the Arab Sufis challenged the rationally apparent and stressed the intuitive, esoteric and visionary instead, Rimbaud challenged the rationalist dualism of Descartes, which had paved the way for Western objectivism and scientific knowledge. His *lettre du voyant* (visionary letter) clearly demonstrated his opposition to the Descartian concept, 'I think, therefore I am', when he wrote, 'I is another' (*Je est un autre*). We might coin another phrase and say, as the Sufis do, 'I think, therefore I am not I'.

Poetry is this journey into the unknown in which the I disappears in a frenzy of ecstasy. It becomes existence, the we and the he: it becomes I and not I.

2. The second characteristic of Rimbaud's text, which is anchored in Western language, is its constant flight from the Western void/the Euclidean-Descartesian void, which places constraints on daily life, in innumerable and diverse ways. We all know how Rimbaud struggled continuously throughout his life to escape from these constraints.

3. The third characteristic of Rimbaud's text is that it transcends the rationalism of Descartesian dualism (subject/object), which is sustained by a tendency to doubt and disclaims poetic knowledge-true knowledge. It is necessary to emphasize what

has been agreed upon by the 'heart'. It is necessary to merge with the lively energy of existence, through the unity of existence. It is necessary to have a transparent vision of the world the inner depths of which conceal lies beyond reason and logic and beyond essence and objectivism.

Poetic knowledge is Sufism; it is the inner knowledge of what we cannot see of the invisible world, of that initial state in which there is no separation between the I and existence and the I and the we. Thus, Rimbaud's text should be read in the same way as Sufi texts are read, if we are to understand it: we must understand the allusion, before we can understand the expression. Al-Hallaj said, 'Those who do not understand what we are alluding to will not be guided by our writings.' Reading such a text therefore is a form of mystical knowledge, a form of intuition.

Thus it is possible to say, incidentally, that any criticism of Rimbaud's text, in the same way as any criticism of Sufi text, is reductive; it is a veil that masks the original light in the text, since it disregards the allusions in their entirety and concentrates on the expression.

4. Rimbaud's text is characterized, like Sufi texts, by its revelation of a prophetic, visionary stance. The West regards the universe as an object that has to be struggled against, while Sufism sees it as an object of harmony. While the West employs reason to comprehend the universe, Sufism uses understanding and intuition. The former regards the universe as an external object while the latter sees it as internal presence – the heart and the core. The meaning of the universe is intertwined with its essence and the meaning of its existence. It is personal and not objective. In this way, the Sufi becomes one with the universe, while the West separates itself from it. The Sufis derive their creative energy from this essence. The universe cannot be known by pure intellect or abstract reason, but only through living and realizing it. Existence is not just a rational issue, but a message. The meaning of

prophecy, which is intrinsically non-Western, is revealed in this. The universe is not a gift to mankind but a charge. Man is entrusted with the universe in which he lives, and his duty is to make it real – to make real 'its absent life'. For thought, according to this vision, does not exist except through being alive. And the basic point at issue, therefore is realization – practice, not theorizations and abstraction.

7

But what path does Rimbaud pursue to bring this about? Before attempting to answer this question, we should recall Rimbaud's short life and think of it as a continuous journey: internal movement linked to external movement, which brings to mind the Sufi *tariqa* (way) and *salik* (spiritual path): a disconnected chain that it is difficult to weave into a solid piece of cloth. A contradictory collection. Sudden flights and escapes. Unexpected paths. It is the same path as that followed by the Sufi, which takes him into the unknown. For it takes time to rid oneself of what is known – the sayings and concepts, the way they are expressed and their basic values. The first step to achieving that is by suspending the action of senses. In his poem *Morning of Intoxication* (*Illuminations*), Rimbaud follows the various stages of the Sufi disciple: entreating the named being (God), taking narcotics (hashish) and so becoming intoxicated, which leads to a suspension of the senses, rejection of dual values (good and evil) and finally the delirium of joy and purity (*fana'*, extinction).

In letters to Georges Izembard (13 May 1871) and Paul Demeny, he describes in detail what pursuing such a path entails. In the first letter, he writes, 'I want to be a poet, and I am working on becoming a visionary. You will never understand and perhaps I do not know how to make it clear to you. The question is attaining what is unknown by a derailment of all the senses. The sufferings are dreadful but I must be strong, so that I will be born a poet, and I shall realize that I am a poet. This is not my fault at all. It is wrong to say: I think. You should say: I am thought. Excuse the play on words. I is the other. I am sorry for the wood that finds itself a violin and I despise those who are unconscious, who quibble about things about which they are completely ignorant.'

In the second letter, Rimbaud writes: 'The proper study of a man who wants to be a poet is to know himself, totally; he seeks his own soul, inspects it, tries it, learns it. Since he knows it, he should educate it. I say that he must make himself a visionary; a man must be a visionary.

'The poet makes himself *voyant* by a long, immense and calculated derailment of all the senses. Unspeakable torture, in which he needs all the faith, all the superhuman strength he can get, by which he becomes the great invalid, the great criminal, the great pariah, above all others – and the supreme Savant! – for he attains the unknown!

'So the poet is truly the fire-stealer. He is responsible for humanity, even for animals. He must invent something that can be touched, felt, heard. If what he brings back from out there has a form, he gives it a form. If it is formless, he gives it a non-form. He will find a language. As any speech is thought, so the turn of universal language will come. It will be a language of the soul for the soul.'

Rimbaud's musings in these two letters are almost the literal equivalent, in modern language, of what is said by the Sufi Arabs. He calls on poets again for forms and ideas, through which the poems he yearns for can be realized. He assesses the poets who have preceded him as follows: Lamartine, 'who was sometimes a visionary but was strangled in the ancient form'; Hugo, 'a very stubborn man who was a true visionary in his last volumes, for *Les Misérables* is a true poem'; Musset, 'who did not know how to do anything. Everything he did was French in that it was extremely hateful.' Second-generation romantics such as Gautier, Leconte de Lisle and de Banville are very visionary, 'because inspecting what is invisible and hearing what cannot be heard is completely different from recalling the spirit of things dead, so Baudelaire was the first visionary, the king of poets, a true god.'

This assessment further confirms Rimbaud's poetic vision and poetic project. When we abolish the action of the senses, we abolish what separates us from the profound essence of things. At that point, life appears to be in total harmony and man and nature appear as one. In this environment, direct living relationships flourish between created beings, and everything that separates man from man and everything that lacks original innocence ceases.

In the context of his research into the realm of the unknown, Rimbaud writes about man ('Vagabonds', *Poésies*, Paris, Gallimard, 1973, p. 177): 'In all thoughtful sincerity, in reality, I had to return him to his primary state, as a son of the sun.' Through the suspension of the senses, i.e. by confusing both the order of knowledge and the order of life, which he describes as 'the disarray of the soul', which is 'something sacred', man is freed from the straitjacket of institutionalism, in whatever form it takes, be it social, religious, cultural or moral ('Alchimie du verbe', 'Délires', ibid., pp. 134, 139). Why are those who reject the dominant morality considered wild?, Rimbaud asks ('Mauvais sang'). This question opens up a gulf between him and the representatives of the dominant religious and cultural order: the clergy, the professors and teachers. 'In the same way, a road opens up, which leads to the original and natural state. In this climate, it is possible for love to be born – a new, universal love, a love that has to be reinvented' ('Délires', 'Vierge', *ibid.,* p. 166, 'A une Raison folle'). With love, it is possible to change life. With love, souls become more transparent, more able to infuse into each other. For love is understanding and altruism and this is what arouses a desire for change in man. Rimbaud therefore vehemently rejects anything that interposes itself in the way of change and anything in particular that transforms religion into a tool of subjugation.

In Rimbaud's eyes the poet, like the Sufi, is someone who is tormented internally, rejected by society and cast out by the morality of 'religious orthodoxy' but who accepts this reality and his punishment. For the method that leads you to the truth does not come from the social order, but from the other, which pierces it – an order that orthodoxy itself regards as an outsider and considers to be insane. The Sufi, like the visionary poet, has a superior knowledge of how to gauge the truth, but when it comes to gauging the social or orthodox external, he is an unbeliever and cursed.

In his poetry, Rimbaud attempts, like the Sufis, to represent what it is impossible to realize ordinarily. It is at one and the same time the end of established life, of the known, and a journey to the depths of being to explore the unknown. This journey is a secret path, in which the poet, like the Sufi, is inculcated with mysteries. Rimbaud's writing is merely a place in which this mystery is revealed. What Rimbaud refers to as 'the alchemy of words' is no more than a tool that enables him to create expressive forms, which are applicable to the secret or the unknown. The path that Rimbaud describes resembled the *mi'raj* (ascent to the path of knowledge) of Sufi terminology. Knowledge here is visionary and reason has nothing to do with it. It lies outside the bounds of what is familiar and normal.

In the light of this it is possible to say that Rimbaud's poetical experience is a form of mystical, symbolic practice. It is based on proscribed methods, which require a huge effort and entail much suffering; nevertheless, he perseveres and realizes his goal of becoming a visionary poet; it is if he is saying: out of death comes life, out of darkness and ignorance, spring forth order and knowledge.

Thus Rimbaud, like the Sufi, appears to reject the manifest world, asserting that poetry is a disclosure of the true and absent life, the invisible. The rejection of this world requires him to reject its system of knowledge, i.e. it requires him to suspend his system of speaking and expression.

Taking Rimbaud as an example, this means that the task of the mystic (the Sufi), i.e. the visionary poet, does not lie in describing visible things, but in piercing through them to see what cannot be seen. For creation is like a form of secret code, whose symbols are solved by the poet. The things are themselves symbols. Light, for example, is something that cannot be expressed in a word. As a word, it means more than its being light; it is the truth, it is God.

To put it another way, the poet's task is to rewrite the world according to the way he understands this secret code. To rename the world. This explains what Rimbaud means by the alchemy of words and by attributing colours to letters. It enables language to apply to the things that it reveals; that is, it enables it to give new names to the world and to its things.

The world can be read from a different angle once the senses are suspended, i.e. once the senses are abandoned, which are able only to produce a reading based on how the perceptible relates to the perceptible, in the realm of the known. In fact, suspending the senses liberates them. At the same time, it liberates the world from its dominant image – from its written existence. Looking at it as something written means looking at it as something fixed or dead. We must free it from this script and chain; we must release it – by so doing we are returning it to the position it held before writing, i.e. to orality. In orality, it reacquires its vitality. The great thinkers of mankind taught orally. Their teachings, which are written down, die if they are not read in ever-changing ways. Such teachings do not provide us with the truth about anything but only help us to discover it. It is a moveable organic truth, which must be constantly reinterpreted if it is to continue to live. It is the same with the world: it is not given to man so that he can enchain it in limited knowledge, but it is given to him so that he can interpret it. Heraclitus describes the world as a river, in which we never swim twice. A great book is similar. When we embark on a book, determining the meaning of every word and applying our finite knowledge to what it says, we kill it. Every reader, through the ages, must start the book as if plunging into a river. When he returns to it a second time, he will interpret it differently, he will have changed and the book will have changed. The book is the person who is reading or interpreting it. The book is not only what the writer writes; the reader also plays his part in it.

8

The suspension of the senses is accompanied by two explosions of knowledge: the explosion of the I and the explosion of language.

According to Rimbaud, the first manifestation – the explosion of the I – occurs when the consciousness of existence and non-existence are revealed together and at the same instant. For the I think/cogito of Rimbaud, if this expression is true, is the opposite of Descartes' expression (*Cogito ergo sum*). It is, more properly, the cogito of the Sufi.

*Je est un autre* ('I is an other') means that existence, as far as the subject is concerned, is something and, as far as the object is concerned, is something completely different. Existence is itself and something apart at the same time, like the example of the I which is the I and the other at the same time.

This shatters the classical dialectical and psychological concept of the oneness of the I or the oneness of the essence. Identity disintegrates. In this disintegration, we discover that the I, in the prevailing ancient sense of the word, has been formed by traditions or social, historical, religious and cultural usage, through its surrender to the world of phenomena. This I is in reality no more than a store in which the fantasies of society, the world of laws or the world of orthodox religious law, as the Sufis regard it, are kept. It conceals the values of society and its heritage, its beliefs and its way of understanding.

While we believe that the I is the I and nothing else apart from that, the essence has a singular oneness and a special identity. The system of meaning is based on traditional logic. But since we have discovered that the one is not the one but is the other, so the fundamental concept of identity in the traditional sense of the word is shaken up and no longer exists. It follows that the thing can be itself and the other. Man can be God in any sense of the word or vice versa. Thus the system of meaning is overturned.

The explosion of the I is nothing but an explosion of expression or explosion of language.

The system of expression or speech, in the framework of our immediate, manifest world, is what the traditional, apparent I practised, and is a system imposed by establishment, usage and consensus. The system of expression employed by the invisible I negates everything that is established. It attempts to glean the unknown, the abstract, the dynamic, that which is beyond tradition and customary usage.

Piercing the world of the manifest cannot be achieved except by piercing its established language. Thus it is possible for us to attain something new by using a new language. In this sense, we see how a new form of poetry can be achieved only by destroying the established and habitual system of meaning and how we can arrive at the truth only by going beyond the orthodox.

This is the internal or mystical project, which aspires to perceive what is not perceived. It gives expression to its essence in what in Sufism is called delirium (*nashwa*), intoxication (*sukr*) or ecstasy (*inkhitaf*), when the I, which is the other, is revealed. In such a state of delirium, the Sufi achieves oneness or unity and publicly proclaims, 'I am God'; in this state of delirium, the Sufi becomes aware of knowledge that has escaped knowledge. So, as much as identity is shaken and we dream that the I is the other, we are able to reach the invisible and to hear the inaudible, as Rimbaud says in his letter to Demeny (ibid., p. 201). Writing here is merely a stabilization of vertigo, as Rimbaud says, 'I fixed vertigoes'. In his writing, Rimbaud frequently uses words that have a symbolic Sufi meaning, such as thirst, drink, quench one's thirst, hunger, eat, nourishment, tears, weeping and laughter, dance and madness. These are words that translate the poet's desire to become one with existence or submit to nature, as we say today. As the Sufi offers himself to God, the poet offers himself to the sun. This symbolizes fusion with the original light of the world and its fire, and emancipation from all forms, in the same way as the Sufi becomes one with the divine presence ('Mauvais sang' and 'Soleil et chair').

The explosion in language, which is the word picture of the explosion of the I, resembles the eruption into words of the ecstatic pronouncement or *shath,* as it is known in Arab Sufism. According to Sufi definition, the *shath* are words translated by the tongue to describe a love that cannot be contained or an extraordinary expression used to describe a passion that overflows by force, in which feelings and excitement boil over. It gives expression to the condition of the seer, whether he is in the presence of the unknown or whether he feels that he is united with it. In such a state, it is not the seer who is speaking or thinking, but a secret, which is uttered by the tongue of the seer. Not the I – rather the unknown, i.e. the hidden oneness between the I and the world. In such a state, the poet, like the Sufi, nullifies the I, but the mystery, the oneness remains. *Shath* is a kind of delirium of the being as a whole, not just of its material body. It is a particular kind of delirium, which is distinct from intoxication or hallucination or delusion or illusion. It goes beyond time and place at the same time.

We can equally name this state insanity, which helps us to understand the words of the Sufi, al-Shibli, which Rimbaud and all other visionary poets have repeated in their own particular way: 'My madness spared me and his reason killed him.' The him refers to al Hallaj.

9

I will conclude these remarks by saying that, while Rimbaud represented a new departure in Western culture, this was only partly true as far as Arab-Eastern culture was concerned, i.e. he was innovatory in the way he composed and explained the elements of his poetry, which was made up of ancient elements, but written in a new format. This is a particular type of pure originality, rather it is the true type; if originality is used to denote a form of creativity, which does not rebel against the old and used, then it is used incorrectly and does not exist. For originality such as this is only a fantasy.

To be truly creative, you must select different elements and put them together, fusing them into a different structure and giving them a special shape. What is conclusive historically is not the finding of an element but what you do with it and how you use it.

I would like to repeat that Rimbaud's poetic inner knowledge is the same as Sufi inner knowledge. It goes against forms of Western rational knowledge. Such perception does not convey a limited and direct knowledge of the world or God or man, but rather opens up a way of understanding them. Knowledge here is taste (experience) or it is personal exploration, which cannot be conveyed and sometimes defies description. Thus, in Rimbaud's writing, we do not find narrow definitions, but rather a collection of possibilities, whose meaning is reinterpreted by each reader and in every age.

## 10

As Rimbaud is a Sufi in the way he uses words, he is also a Sufi in his use of silence. There is no speech except between self and other, and in order for there to be words, there must be a distinction between the subject and the object. The visionary poet (or the Sufi) attains the furthermost limit in his journey towards the unknown, that is, he reaches a state that cannot be expressed in words, which is the state of non-speaking. The search for delirium, i.e. oneness with the unknown, leads to a form of liquefaction between the subject and the object, to an equivocal state, which can be described as being, which is neither subject nor object.

This connection cannot be achieved with words, nor are words a means to it. It is like the connection of love: delirium and oneness. It is utter bliss: the closed being opens up to himself and dissolves into the other. This perfect connection severs the established chain, since fixed concepts stop and their words come to an end. There is complete freedom in this oneness. Silence here is the silence of supreme delirium. It is impossible to describe it. The action of speaking fails. It is the moment of joy, the moment of achieving unity with the original being or the discovery of eternity, as Rimbaud says (ibid., p. 145):

> It is rediscovered!
> What? Eternity
> Is the sea mingled with the sun.

The significance of dance among the Sufis lies in this state of non-speech. Chaos becomes holy in it. I believe that the reason for Rimbaud's silence, his transference to a state of non-speaking, as far as his poetry was concerned, can be explained by that. But that is another question. (He stopped writing poetry in 1875, as he mentioned in the first of his letters from Aden, 17 August 1880.)

In this state of non-speaking, we can say in the internal language of the Sufi, 'The limits of paradise are my body.' This conflicts with the establishment orthodox view, which says, 'True life is what is absent from this ephemeral world; it is impossible (to have it) except in the other world and it is especially for the believers who are without fault.' 'Deliverance is a sign of a more beautiful and truer other world, and in it man will find eternal life.' 'I hope for life tomorrow and will bear the torment of the present with patience.'

The Sufis say, 'We must pursue happiness, that is, Sufi happiness, now.' Attainment of death, i.e. the other, is only the attainment of perfect happiness. For happiness begins here and now, and so does eternity. The state of oneness is in fact paradise, before paradise. Eternity does not wait and can only be lived. For death is only a prolonged state of oneness, the final state, which is the last return for the complete being. This is what allows us to understand how the I, which is also the other, dissolves into all created beings. For God is existence in its entirety. And the I is existence in its entirety as well.'

Rimbaud says, 'I have become Opera' (ibid.), which is a symbol of this oneness. In a further symbol of this oneness, Ibn 'Arabi says, 'My heart became a receptacle for every image.'

In this framework we can understand Rimbaud's disintegration and his decision to travel and trade. It is as if he is living al-Niffari's words: 'If you do not witness what cannot be said, you will shatter what can be said.'

We agree with what David Guerdon says, when he describes Rimbaud's life as representing Sufi oneness: 'the systematic wish of controlled development towards a certain goal since his childhood – in unity and satisfaction. So Rimbaud the gunrunner is also the adolescent poet, fulfilling his fate but with other ways and tools' ('L'Itinéraire alchimique d'Arthur Rimbaud', in *Rimbaud Multiple*, eds D. Bedou and J. Touzot, Paris, 1986, p. 100).

So let us end by reporting Rimbaud's own words from *Les Illuminations*, which is the crowning achievement of his poetic project and which liberates man and returns him to himself, to his original condition, 'a son of the sun'. Let us say 'in the splendid setting, which surrounds the whole of the east, I completed my huge work, and I have lived in my well-known retirement' (ibid., *Hayawat 3*, p. 164).

In Fariduddin Attar's *Conference of the Birds*, thirty birds discover the amazing Simorgh bird after a long journey of pilgrimage, and they learn that it is they; they have merged into each other. They have one identity but many images.

Muhyiddin ibn 'Arabi says, 'Whoever sees you from where he is, sees only himself.' So in order to know the other, you must see it from where it is, not from where you are. It seems to me that from this point of view as well, that of dialogue between the self and the other, and between cultures, Rimbaud is a founding force. He sees Sufism, i.e. the East, as the other, from where the East is not from where he is.

# Extracts from Surrealist Writing

## General Thoughts

Surrealism is pure, psychic automatism by which it is intended to express, verbally, in writing or in any other way, the true function of thought, thought dictated in the absence of all control exerted by reason and outside all aesthetic or moral preoccupations.

Surrealism (philosophy) is based on a belief in the superior reality of certain forms of association hitherto neglected, in the omnipotence of the dream and in the disinterested play of thought. It leads to the permanent destruction of all other psychic mechanisms and to its substitution for them in the solution of the principal problems of life.

André Breton, *First Surrealist Manifesto*, 1924 (Paris, Gallimard, 1973, *Pensées*, p. 37).

Everything leads to the belief that there exists a certain point of the mind at which life and death, the real and the imaginary, the past and the future, the communicable and the incommunicable, the high and the low, are not perceived as contradictions. It would be vain to attribute to surrealism any other motive than the hope of determining this point.

André Breton, *What Is Surrealism?*, Brussels, Henri Keener, 1934. See also Henri Béhar and Michel Carassou, *Surréalisme: Textes et Discussions*, Paris, Librairie Générale Française, 1984, p. 6.

Surrealism in the widest sense of the word represents the most recent attempt to break with existing things and to put others in their place, which are fully effective and functioning and whose moving contours are implicitly inscribed in the depths of their being ... never before in France has a school of poets brought together in such a way, and so very consciously, the critical issues of poetry and existence.

Marcel Raymond, as quoted in Béhar and Carassou, Paris, 1984, p. 7.

Breton used to distinguish between eternal surrealism, whose origins can be found in all cultures, and the surrealism that historically assumed a concrete form in France between 1924 (the date of the First Manifesto) and 1969 (the date of the dissolution of the Surrealist Group) three years after his death. The relationship between the two is constant. Historical surrealism is fed by the springs of eternal surrealism in the same way as the latter is revived by the presence of sensitive beings.

Ibid., p. 8.

Through such literary influences, surrealism finds a means of thinking and a logic that is non-Descartesian and allows it to adopt the magic mentality. The more it is aware of its spiritual relationship with children, primitive peoples and the insane, the more it will extend its curiosity to other ethnic groups among civilizations with an esoteric tradition.

Ibid., p. 8.

Nothing can prevent us from talking about a surrealist humanity ...
It is a matter of breaking down the walls that limit the individual,
estranging him from himself. Surrealism refuses such obstacles and
binary opposites (intellect-insanity, reality-fantasy, child-adult,
wakefulness-dream ...). It decrees an original humanity, which
recalls its individuality in a constant state of creativity and creation.

Ibid., p. 9.

## Love

The true revolution for Surrealists is the victory of desire.

Maurice Nadeau, as quoted in Béhar and Carassou, p. 120.

In their struggle for freedom, the Surrealists regarded Eros as a
subversive and negative force, which had to be brandished against
a repressive reality.

Béhar and Carassou, p. 124.

Surrealist love emanates from sensuality, which an expectation of
happiness arouses and which does not stop at the limits of satisfying
the senses alone.

Ibid., p. 132.

Love plays no part in the tyranny of enchained instincts. The
heartfelt passion of beings is to live a unique love (*un amour fou*).
But social constraints and material considerations (the colonnades
of minutes, hours and days which follow each other but have no
resemblance to each other) risk making of this unique love an
exciting aspiration rather than a lived reality.

Ibid., p. 134.

Without touching upon the use of means that the transformation of the world necessitates, and which are notably the suppression of those social obstacles, it is perhaps not useless to convince oneself that the idea of a unique love proceeds from a mystical attitude – something which does not exclude the fact that it is entertained by actual society for its equivocal ends. I believe that I can glimpse a possible synthesis between the idea and its opposite.

André Breton, L'Amour fou, Paris, Gallimard, 1936, pp. 85–86;<br>as quoted in Béhar and Carassou, p. 134.

This quest for an elective love, which excludes any narcissism, will lead to the celebration of the beloved, even if she is not yet more than a woman who is dreamed about and expected as in Free Union [a poem by Breton] ... The poet becomes submerged in the beloved. Everything that can be awaited from outside and from within becomes reconciled in a single being.

André Breton, as quoted in Béhar and Carassou, p. 137.

And yet, woman, you take the place of all forms. You are the epitome of a marvellous world, of the natural world, and when I close my eyes, it is you who are reborn. You are the wall and the breach. You are the horizon and the presence ... the total eclipse and the light. How can you think of anything that is not a miracle, when the miracle is there in its nocturnal robe? So for me the universe gradually fades away, melts, while from its depths arises an adorable phantom; there ascends a woman larger than life, whose outline is at last clear, who, with nothing separating her from me, appears everywhere in the most positive guise of an expiring world ... The woman, larger than life, is growing still larger. Now the world is her portrait ... Mountains, you will never be anything but this woman's distant background and, if I am present in the foreground, it is so that she shall have a forehead on which to lay her hand. She is growing. Already the appearance of the sky has been tainted by this growing magician. Her dishevelled traces cause comets to tumble into goblets. Her hands, but everything I touch talks of her hands. Behold, I am nothing more than a drop of rain on her skin, a drop of dew. Sea, do you really love the putrescent corpses of your drowned victims? Do you love the softness of their facile limbs? Do you love their abjuring lover from the unfathomed deep? Their incredible purity and their floating hair? Then, my ocean, love me. Pass across my palms, water like tears, boundless woman by whom I am entirely bathed. Pass across my sky, my silence and my veils. Let my birds lose themselves in your eyes.

Louis Aragon, *Le paysan de Paris*, Paris, Gallimard, 1926, translated by Simon Watson Taylor as *Paris Peasant*, London, Jonathan Cape, 1971; as quoted in Béhar and Carassou, pp. 138–39.

André Breton wanted to justify 'lyrical comportment/behaviour', and often called for it. He and his poet friends provided many examples of it, in which they celebrated woman and, through her, love, which allowed for/brought about the accomplishment of the miracle.

Béhar and Carassou, p. 139.

> The stars become you, clouds imagine you
> …
> I sing with great joy that I am singing about you
> The artlessness of waiting for you, the innocence of knowing you.
> You, the one who curbs forgetfulness, hope and ignorance,
> You suppress absence and bring me into the world.
> I sing to sing, I love you to sing
> The mystery in which love creates me and is delivered.

Paul Eluard, 'Capitale de la douleur', *Œuvres complètes*, Paris, Bibliothèque de la Pléiade, Gallimard, 1968, pp. 140–41; as quoted in Béhar and Carassou, pp. 139–140.

A surrealist vision of woman emerges out of the poems of Breton, Eluard, Aragon and Peret, a woman who is illuminated and illuminates. She reveals man to himself at the same time as she unveils the secrets of the universe.

In that she represents everything that is real, woman is also nature, the consoling mother, the muse and the mediator.

Béhar and Carassou, p. 142.

I believe that there are two types of women who are suited to experience of sublime love because they personify two aspects of femininity in clearly discernible ways, which distinguish them from the others. They are the child-woman and the enchantress; the child-woman represents an optimistic expression of love and the enchantress its pessimistic face.

The child-woman arouses the love of the wholly virile man because she completes him trait for trait. This love reveals her to herself and projects her into a marvellous world, to which she abandons herself entirely. She resembles life at its climax, spring bursting with flowers and song ... She waits for love as a bird waits the sun and welcomes it in a present she does not hope for, but which is more sumptuous than anything she could have dreamed of.

Benjamin Peret, as quoted in Béhar and Carassou, pp. 143–44.

'The child-woman is the one who imposes herself on the surrealist imagination and the texts of Breton', in which 'his thought evolves human characteristics through child-woman'.

Ibid., pp. 145–46.

We should not forget the importance Breton ascribes to childhood, which he sees as a symbol of 'true life'.

Béhar and Carassou, p. 146.

Throughout his poetry, Paul Eluard celebrates the single being who ends by merging into 'a reality which words and thoughts are unable to attain'. The quest for love fuses with the oneness. In this sense, love takes on a mythical dimension.

Ibid., p. 149.

Sublime love is called to make the human being divine ... It represents the revolt of an individual against religion and society.

Benjamin Peret, as quoted in Béhar and Carassou, p. 150.

The woman takes the place of the Absolute, in such a conception.

Béhar and Carassou, p. 150.

I stress that physical love and spiritual love are one.

André Breton, as quoted in Béhar and Carassou, p. 152.

The coming together of the two lovers to form a perfect whole allows them to create the universe just as the universe created them.

Robert Benayoun, as quoted in Béhar and Carassou, p. 153.

In an act of complete fusion, the man, reconciled with himself and with the world, once again becomes a 'microcosm', 'a summary of the universe'.

Ibid.

## Reason/Imagination

We are still living under the reign of logic, but the logical processes of our time apply only to the solution of problems of secondary interest. The absolute rationalism, which remains in fashion, allows only those facts narrowly relevant to our experience to be considered ... Needless to say, boundaries have been assigned even to experience. In the guise of civilization, under the pretext of progress, we have succeeded in dismissing from our minds anything that, rightly or wrongly, could be regarded as superstition or myth; and we have proscribed every way of seeking the truth that does not conform to convention.

André Breton, as quoted in Béhar and Carassou, p. 158.

The Surrealists regard reason as the most powerful enemy of the spirit.

*Ibid., p. 159.*

As far as we young Surrealists were concerned, reason was the great 'prostitute'. We believed that followers of Descartes and Voltaire and other members of the intelligentsia had done nothing but hang on to established and obsolete values while affecting a façade of non-conformism. Since the end of the winter of 1924, we had abandoned ourselves frenetically to automatism and the game ... I would add objectively that the game – the serious game ... – added to this immersion in the night (in what German Romantics call the nocturnal side of things) and the desirable summons of the marvellous.

*André Masson, as quoted in Béhar and Carassou, p. 159.*

That the facts of life appear coherent is the result of a process of accommodation, which resembles oneness, which makes thought appear coherent, while its free functioning is pure intolerance.

*Salvador Dalí, as quoted in Béhar and Carassou, p. 160.*

In the abstract desert, rationality bursts forth in the expressions of Dalí (with liquid pleasure). Tangible irrationality wells up. For if this tangible reality appears irrational, then it is solely the fault of reason. This arrogant and passé reason has ended up by assuming such restrictive forms that the spirit in the course of these last few years has had to declare itself opposed to it. Paralysed and paralysing, it places its opacity between the thinker seated in order to think and the matter in motion, the matter in the process of change, as if this matter were not matter for thought. Reason, this pawn, soils everything with its cautious reality. Intellectuals do not like risk.

*René Crével, as quoted in Béhar and Carassou, p. 161.*

Logic freezes the representations of the world into a series of contradictions – the real and the possible, the action and the dream, normality and madness, constituting the apparel of social conservatism, which is destined to ward off any strange behaviour by the individual.

Béhar and Carassou, p. 161.

Imagination is the only thing that works. Nothing, neither strict logic nor overwhelming impression, has the power to make me convinced about reality, nor convince me that I am not basing it on a delirium of interpretation.

Aragon, *Paris Peasant*, as quoted in Béhar and Carassou, p. 162.

For imagination, which we all possess, is alone able to lift the embargo from the areas that we are unable to enter except through it. It alone has the power to banish 'the phallus of logic'.

Béhar and Carassou, p. 162.

What I love best in you, beloved Imagination, is that you do not grant pardon. The single word of freedom is the only thing that still makes me rejoice. We make a slave of imagination … This is how we escape from everything we find in the depths of our being, from supreme justice. Imagination alone demonstrates what is possible and that is sufficient to halt, if only for a little, the terrible forbidden, and sufficient for me to abandon myself to it without fear of being wrong.

André Breton, as quoted in Béhar and Carassou, p. 163.

## Automatic Writing

The process of automatic writing is not restricted to language. Automatism also brings revelations about man and about the regions of thought 'where desire without constraint is based'.

Béhar and Carassou, p. 178.

Automatic writing constantly unlocks new doors to the unconscious, and bit by bit, as it confronts the conscious and the world, it adds to its treasure. It is also possible in the same way for it to renew this consciousness and this world by delivering them from the atrocious conditions that are imposed on them, and lightens their oppression on the individual.

Paul Eluard; as quoted in Béhar and Carassou, p. 179.

Automatic writing has remained the most frequently used method of exploring the unconscious, though other methods have been experimented with.

Béhar and Carassou, p. 179.

It is not the requirements of sly criticism, particularly attentive and aggressive on this form (automatic writing), that have prevented me from recognizing that over the years I have counted on the torrential discharge of automatic writing for the definitive cleansing of the literary stable. In this respect, the desire to throw open the locks will doubtless remain the generating idea of the surrealists.

André Breton, as quoted in Béhar and Carassou, p. 179.

It is natural that what appears first in this encounter between poetry and unreflected writing is the decision to escape from its constraints. Reason keeps watch over us. Critical thought keeps its hold on us. Our speech is based on custom and convention. Automatic writing reveals a means of writing out of reach of these forces, ... which frees it from the mundane, and its boring view. The freedoms in writing in the history of Surrealism can be compared to the experiences of sleep ...

Automatic writing is intended to suppress constraint and get rid of intermediaries, to repel any intervention, to place the hand that is writing in contact with something original, making out of this active hand a sovereign passivity, no more than a 'pen-hand', an instrument, a slavish tool, an independent power over which no one has complete control, which belongs to no one, which no longer can do or know anything other than write: a dead hand is analogous to this hand of glory of which magic speaks. That's what automatic writing means to us above all else. The language that it offers us is not the language of authority. It has no power of speech. It is not at all the language I speak. In it, 'I' never speaks. One of the characteristics of daily speech is that understanding is part of its nature. But at this point of the experience, the language is not one that can be understood. In this lies the risk of the poetic function. The poet is someone who understands a language, without being understood it.

Maurice Blanchot, as quoted in Béhar and Carassou, pp. 181–83.

## Dream

Since time immemorial, the dream has been seen as a form of inspiration. Gods speak to their victims in dreams. Nevertheless, we should observe that those people who carefully note down their dreams, unshackled by any literary or medical preoccupations ... don't do so to set up a relationship with something supernatural. One can say that, while dreaming, they feel themselves less inspired than ever. They report with a faithful objectivity what they remember dreaming. One can even say that nowhere is there greater objectivity than in the recital of dreams. For here nothing interposes between reality and sleep as reason, censure etc do in wakefulness.

Aragon, as quoted in Béhar and Carassou, p. 187.

… The dream is the only thing that allows man to have complete freedom. Thanks to the dream, death no longer has an obscure meaning and life takes on a different sense.

… What are paper and pen? What are writing and poetry when faced with this giant whose muscles are bound up by the muscles of the clouds?

… Surrealism opens the doors of dreams to all those for whom the night is miserly. Surrealism lies at the crossroads of the enchantment of sleep, alcohol, tobacco, ether, opium, cocaine, morphine, but it is also the breaker of chains. We don't sleep, we don't drink, we don't drug, but we dream and the flickering of the lamps introduces marvellous sponges decorated with gold, into our brains.

P. Eluard, J. A. Boiffard and R. Vitrac, as quoted in Béhar and Carassou, p. 189.

I do not believe that the dream is the exact opposite of thought. What I know of it inclines me to believe that it is a freer and more abandoned form of thought.

Pierre Reverdy, as quoted in Béhar and Carassou, p. 189.

It was at the time when the Surrealists were most deeply engaged in political action that they most vehemently defended the rights of the dreamer. Surrealism put itself at the service of the revolution, because revolution serves dreams.

Béhar and Carassou, p. 189.

Were it not for night charging itself with effacing the intrigues and obstacles, and choosing for him what he needs to survive, the solitary individual, caught up in strange crowds, constant hostile attacks and the turbulence of sensation and ideas, would not be able to survive.

Maxime Alexander, as quoted in Béhar and Carassou, p. 191.

Automatic writing, dream narration, simulations of delirium – the techniques to investigate the unconscious were employed simultaneously or one after the other and allowed the discovery of the dynamics of the imagination. It is perhaps with this idea of concrete irrationality that the function of consciousness and the function of desire appear the most intimately mixed. Falling into unconsciousness favours a deepening of the reality, which is also its invention. The boundaries of the world are pushed back because at the same time, this world is recreated. The objective and the subjective are no longer separate.

Béhar and Carassou, p. 203.

## What Lies Behind Reality?

The demands of the process as much as the circumstances that led them to prioritize the action meant that Surrealists knew they should avoid the dangers of mystical romanticism and skirt a reality which would have made them founder in the nihilism of despair. At the same time, they did not regard the dream as a refuge beyond the limits of a world that was unable to satisfy the individual, but instead regarded it as a stimulus, which would not so much compel the individual to be satisfied with his condition as help him overcome it with all the strength he had regained.

Surrealism, in the same movement with which it explores the depths of the self, faces the external world, not so much to recognize it as it is as to recreate it according to the laws of desire.

Ibid., pp. 217–18.

Existence is elsewhere.

André Breton, as quoted in Béhar and Carassou, p. 219.

According to Breton, there is a narrow interpenetration between natural necessity, which orders the world, and human necessity, through which the profound tendencies of the individual often come to be realized. A reconciliation appears possible between man and the external world since the latter ceases to be regarded as strange or hostile. To arrive at this reconciliation it is necessary for Surrealism to begin by rejecting the reality of the world. This rejection is only the first stage in a dialectic movement, which calls for renewal, just as it attains its ultimate goal – fusion with the world.

Béhar and Carassou, p. 227.

The basis for Surrealism is neither the rationalism of Hegel nor the work of Marx. It is freedom.

Ferdinand Alquié, as quoted in Béhar and Carassou, p. 230.

I demand that people note that Surrealist research along with alchemic research presents a remarkable unity of purpose. The philosopher's stone is nothing other than a thing that should be given to man's imagination to take forcible revenge on everything, and after years of taming the spirit and crazy submission, here we are again, attempting to finally free this imagination by the long, huge, reasoned deregulation of the senses.

André Breton, as quoted in Béhar and Carassou, pp. 251–52.

Between 'high magic' and what Breton is not afraid to call 'high poetry', there appears to exist a profound unity of preoccupation. In 'Alchemic Theatre', Antonin Artaud makes clear the whole range of this meeting between poetic illumination and truths is anchored in tradition.

Béhar and Carassou, p. 252.

Through the practice of their poetry, the Surrealists found the sense of the great alchemic work, which led the disciple into the mysteries of the universe.

Ibid., p. 254.

We know that for those who reduce poetry to verbal jewellery, the word is a mere description of the mundane. But for people who continue to regard poetry as something mysterious, poetry is a 'sacred action'. I mean, by that, that it exceeds the ordinary scheme of things. Like alchemy, it attempts to associate itself with the mystery of 'primordial creation', that is, to accomplish great work within the microcosm.

This explains why transmutation took on a poetic value for the alchemists, which was magical and sacred. Inversely, modern poetry is a form of linguistic transmutation, and those who criticize it do not know what they are talking about when they describe it as alchemy. It seeks to bring about an internal metamorphosis through an external transmutation. In the case of Surrealism, it inaugurates an attempt to change man and universe in bringing together automatic writing and objective chance, the warning signs of clairvoyance and the future glorification of man. Alchemy is poetry, therefore, in the strongest sense of the term, and Surrealism is truly an alchemic transmutation. Both of them have the same goal: the transformation of man and the universe by the transmutation of mineral or verbal matter.

Michel Carrouges, as quoted in Béhar and Carassou, pp. 254–55.

The cognitive approach of Surrealism is corrupted, as it is in alchemy, by a wish to transform man and universe and to return man to his special place, by recovering his lost powers.

Béhar and Carassou, p. 255.

There is no value in a scientific knowledge of nature unless there is contact with nature through poetic and, dare I say, mythic ways.

André Breton, as quoted in Béhar and Carassou, p. 256.

The memory of a lost paradise authorizes man not to be satisfied with the conditions that he is forced to undergo in this world, and provides him with sufficient strength to seek to overcome them.

Béhar and Carassou, p. 256.

We live in the ruins of paradise but from here we will obtain the hope of attaining the supreme point.

Michel Carrouges, as quoted in Béhar and Carassou, p. 256.

Perhaps the Surrealists, by making smooth the desire 'of the great carrier of the keys', risk being forbidden entry into the marvellous world. If his reality is removed from reality, nevertheless desire never ceases to bring it back there. Isn't it then the exaltation of desire – at the same time as the freedom of the individual – that maintains Surrealism at an equal distance from materialism and spiritualism?

Ibid., p. 259.

## Language

Throughout its existence, Surrealism has proclaimed the prime importance of language. Prime importance in time: automatic writing is at the basis of the development of the movement ... and the prime importance attached to language, not only as a means of communication, but also as a means of expression and action, and the two are linked. In substance, the Surrealists say that had we not been betrayed by language we would be able to express ourselves completely without barriers and know ourselves for what we are, beyond social conventions. Were this function of knowing reestablished, men would understand each other immediately and would be able to transform the world together. There is almost a nostalgia in the language, particularly that of Breton, which is similar to that of Rousseau.

Ibid., pp. 311–12.

It is sufficient for our criticism to touch on the laws that preside in their assembly (the words). Doesn't the mediocrity of our universe depend essentially on our power to state it? ... What is it that prevents me from disturbing the word order? ... Language can and must be uprooted from its bondage. No more descriptions about nature, no more studies of customs! Silence so that I can pass to the point that no one has passed. Silence. After you, my beautiful language.

André Breton, as quoted in Béhar and Carassou, p. 314.

Language disappears, as the instrument becomes the subject. Thanks to automatic writing, it is raised to the highest degree. Now it mingles with the 'thoughts' of man; it is linked to the only true form of spontaneity. It is human freedom, effective and apparent. Let rational construction be rejected, let universal meanings disappear into thin air – this means that language must not be used, that it must not serve to express, that it is free, that it is freedom itself.

When Surrealists talk about 'emancipating' words, about treating them as something more than minor auxiliaries, they are talking about a true social quest. There are individuals and a class of people whom others hold as instruments and elements of exchange: in both cases, liberty, the possibility of man to be himself, is directly implicated.

But this emancipation of words can only be with double meanings. For strictly speaking the word is not emancipated in automatic writing but becomes one with my freedom. I slide into the word. It retains my imprint and it is my printed reality. In one way, it is united with my 'non-unity'. In another, this freedom of words means that the words become free in themselves: they no longer exclusively depend on the things they express; rather they act on their own account, they play, and they 'make love', as Breton puts it.

Maurice Blanchot, as quoted in Béhar and Carassou, pp. 326–27.

The Surrealist belief that language is an underground river that they have a duty to bring to light has led them to address the issue of inspiration in terms that are different from those employed by the

Romantics. As they see it, the river belongs to everyone and it is sufficient for man to know how to listen to its murmur, that is, by placing himself in conditions that enable him to hear it.

Béhar and Carassou, p. 328.

The poet is the one who inspires, rather than the one who is inspired.

Paul Eluard, as quoted in Béhar and Carassou, p. 339.

## Writing

The Surrealists are primarily poets. As such they consider the way they express themselves, in particular the image, as an excellent vehicle for poetry. It is not a question of rhetoric, but of life and action, in that the images that appear to them, based on their experience of automatism, appear to be dictated by the unconscious. The poet, in his writing, constructs a bridge from the subjective to the objective, which resonates with the universe and works with its language to change it.

Béhar and Carassou, p. 254.

The image is a pure creation of the spirit. It is not the product of a comparison but a drawing together of two realities, which are to a greater or lesser extent removed from each other. Inasmuch as the relationship of these realities is distant and true, the image will be strong and it will possess an emotive power and poetic reality.

It is not possible to bring together in a useful manner two realities that do not relate to each other ... The strength of an image is not derived from its brutality or fantasy but because the association of ideas is distant and fair ... It is the emotions that are evoked rather than the image, which is the sign of greatness –

such emotions as these are pure and poetic, because they do not originate from imitation, evocation or comparison.

Pierre Reverdy, as quoted in Béhar and Carassou, pp. 354–55.

The force and authenticity of the Surrealist image can be judged according to its unexpectedness, its discontinuity, and the suddenness with which it gushes forth. The image is like a spark both because of its radiance and the way it fades away. The liveliest images are those that disappear the most quickly. The greater the explosive and incoherent character of the image, the more suggestive its power and the better it is able to express the sense of cosmic participation.

M. Eigeldinger, as quoted in Béhar and Carassou, p. 358.

The poem must be the abandonment of the intellect. It cannot be anything else.

Poetry is the antithesis of literature.

Eluard and Breton, as quoted in Béhar and Carassou, p. 375.

# Notes

*Introduction*
1. Guy-René Doumayrou, 'Surréalisme, ésotéricisme', Paris, *Docsur*, no. 8, April 1989. Only 350 copies of this leaflet were printed and it was distributed only among members of the Actuel Society and to some people who had assisted the Society. I would like to extend my thanks here to Abd al-Qadir al-Janabi, who brought the article to my attention.
2. *Entretiens*, Paris, Gallimard, 1952, p. 151.
3. Louis Aragon, 'Une Vague de rêve', *Commerce*, Paris, Autumn 1924.
4. Ibn Taymiyya, 'Letter of Slavery', distributed by al-Maktab al-Islami, Damascus, 1962, p. 26.
5. 'And they drank in their hearts because of their rejection [of the covenant]': Surat of the Cow: 93. 'If they make no answer, know that they are the slaves of their caprices. And who is in greater error than the man who is led by his caprice without guidance from Allah': Surat of the Story: 50. 'The unbelievers follow vain conjectures and the whims of their own souls, although the guidance of their Lord has come to them': Surat of the Star: 23. 'And now we have set you on the right path. Follow it and do not yield to the lust of ignorant men': Surat of Kneeling: 18.
6. 'Letter of Slavery', pp. 27–28.
7. Ibid., p. 30.
8. *Mi'raj al-Wusul*, Cairo, 1387AH, p. 13.
9. Ibid., p. 14.
10. Surrealism was based essentially on a re-examination of Western civilization in the cultural climate that followed the First World War. The movement was founded in Paris in 1924 by four poets: Tristan Tzara, André Breton, Louis Aragon and Philippe Soupault. From its inception, its members derided customs and traditions and demanded 'a change in life'; they

rejected models and values, and extolled life and freedom instead. Their violent rebellion was associated with detailed research into what lay behind the real material world. In this, Surrealism was more than just a literary movement; it was a new way of imagining and understanding reality. In 1924, the Surrealist movement was established in the strict sense of the word and Paul Eluard, Jacques Baron, Robert Desnos, Max Ernst, Roger Vitrac, Gérard de Nerval, André Masson and Antonin Artaud joined the original poets already referred to (see Bartoli-Anglard: *Le Surréalisme*).

11. Michel de Certau, *La fable mystique*, Paris, Gallimard, 1982, p. 411.

*Knowledge*

1. André Breton, *Œuvres complètes*, 1, Paris, Gallimard, 1988.
2. Breton's words, 'The scarecrow of death is a phantasm' (see *The Second Manifesto*), remind us of the *hadith*, 'People sleep and when they die they wake up', as long as we understand death from the Sufi point of view, i.e. death from reason and consciousness. They also remind us of René Char's words, 'If man doesn't close his eyes wilfully, he will end up not seeing what it is desirable to see.'
3. The quotation is cited in Volker Zotz, *André Breton*, Paris, Editions Somogy, 1990.
4. Henri Béhar and Michel Carassou, *Le surréalisme, textes et débats*, Paris, Librairie Générale Française, 1984, p. 159.
5. *Questions de l'esprit visionnaire*, Paris, Albin Michel, 1990, pp. 5–12.
6. Jean-Pierre Bayard, 'L'Expérience visionnaire d'Arthur Rimbaud', in *Questions de l'esprit visionnaire*, no. 82, Paris, Albin Michel, 1990, p. 21.
7. Ibid.
8. Surat Muhammad, v. 34: Will they then not meditate on the Qur'an, or are there locks on the hearts?; Surat of the Weeping Woman, v. 22: As for such, He hath written faith upon their hearts; Surat of the Family of Imra'an, v. 7: But those in whose hearts is doubt pursue, forsooth, that which is allegorical seeking [to cause] dissension by seeking to explain it.
9. See the text concerning the green mountain in Toshihito Izutsu, *The Concept of Perpetual Creation in Islamic Mysticism and Zen Buddhism*. See also the author's analysis of the theory of permanent creation in Buddhism and Islamic mysticism, pp. 85–120.
10. *Kitab Sibawiya*, part 1, p. 7.
11. Ibid., p. 8.

*Love*

1. Ibn 'Arabi defines taste as 'the first principle of revelation', and he says, 'that it is a state, which strikes the servant (of God) suddenly in his heart'. He says that tastes differ according to the different types of revelations; if

a revelation appears in images then the taste will be imaginary, and if it appears in divine and cosmic names, then the taste will be intellectual. He says that taste comes only from revelation. Taste therefore is 'the path of knowing. It is not possible to know what results from taste except through taste, so understanding of this knowledge is restricted to the taster' (see the entry 'dhawq' (taste) in Souad Hakim, *al-Mu'jam al-Sufi* (*A Sufi Lexicon*), Beirut, 1981). Taste literally means testing something by sampling it in your mouth. Everything that has come down to man from disasters, he has tasted. The word is used in two ways, literally (really) and figuratively (in place of another word) (see entries in *Miqyas al-Lughat* and *Lisan al-Arab* dictionaries).

*Writing*

1. Dr Mahmoud al-Ghirab in his book *Love and Divine Love* (Damascus, 1983) provides a comprehensive analysis of Ibn 'Arabi's understanding of love based on his writings, on which I have relied heavily in this chapter. The writings that I refer to are *al-Futuhat, Muhadarat al-Abrar wa Musamarat al-Akhyar, Muwaqi' al-Nujum, Dhakha'ir wa al-'Alaq fi Tarjuman al-Ashwaq, Taj al-Rasa'il wa Minhaj al-Wasa'il' al-Asra' ila Maqam al-Asra* and *al-Tanazzulat al-Mawsiliya* . However, as I am merely presenting a précis of Ibn 'Arabi's words, I do not specify the sources.
2. Abd al-Rahman Badawi read *qadam bila qadam* with a *fatah* or 'a' vowel marking over the qaf, meaning 'the man' (Badawi, *al-Shatahat*, p. 6). In my opinion he is wrong, and the correct way is the one I have followed.
3. *Fana'* (extinction) is the decline of bad qualities, as *baqa'* (permanence) is the existence of good qualities. There are two kinds of *fana'*, one which, as we have just said, can be attained by spiritual practice and the other, which is non-awareness of this world and submersion in the greatness of the creator and seeing God (al-Jurjani, *al-Ta'rifat: al-Fana'*, p. 113).

*The Aesthetic Dimension*

1. The difference between djinn and angels and mankind with respect to their creation is that djinn 'are souls that are inspired with wind; angels, souls that are inspired with light and mankind, souls that are inspired with ghostly apparitions'.
2. Ibn 'Arabi, *al-Futuhat*, vol. 1, Cairo, Othman Yahya, 1972, p. 152.
3. Ibid.
4. Ibid.

*The Writings of al-Niffari or the Poetic of Thought*

1. Sufism rejects the Aristotelian laws of reason, which have held sway in Western culture. They are the three famous laws: the law of identity (*A is A*); the law of contradiction (*A cannot be both A and not A at the same time*);

and the law of the excluded middle (*A must be either A or not A*). There is nothing between existence and non-existence.

### Vision and Image

1. This text was written especially for the Institute of the Arab World, Contemporary Arab Art (Collection of the gallery of the Institute of the Arab World), Paris.
2. The saying that poetry is 'fire without smoke' is also attributed to him.
3. In the theatre the distance between art and reality is much broader. There is a. the original action (concept or allegory of love, for example); b. the human action; c. the language that describes the human action; d. the acting, which imitates what the language describes; e. the seeing. Thus the spectator does not see (live) the love except as a shadow of a shadow of a shadow.
4. It is possible here to present another interpretation of Islam's stand on figuration. Islam is not totally against figuration itself, but it is opposed to it as a veil, that is, as a way of imitating sight and shadow. However, it is not opposed to figuration when it concerns itself with the facts of things and examines their proofs and profound relationships.

### Creativity and Form

1. Translator's note: al-Khalil bin Ahmed al Farahidi originated the concept of *bahr*/metre in Arab verse.

### Rimbaud, Orientalist, Sufi

1. I wrote this text originally as a paper, which I presented at Bologna University, Italy, on the occasion of the third session of the Arab-European University in July 1988 as part of the programme of 'contradictory readings' directed by the writer and novelist Umberto Eco, in which European specialists lectured on Arab works and Arab specialists lectured on European works. It was later published in *Mawaqif* magazine, issue 57, 1989. Here it is republished with some additions and changes.
2. The *qasida* (poem) entitled '*hakaya*' (story) (*Illuminations*, p. 160) is a symbolic essence of what Sharahyar represented in *The Thousand and One Nights*, and the Sufi journey, which Atar described in *Mantiq al-Tir* (Conference of the Birds). Seen from one perspective, the meeting between the prince and the djinni reminds us of *The Thousand and One Nights*. The prince, like Sharahyar, kills all his women. This is the external manifestation of the poem. Seen in another way, the poem represents an internal search: an internal journey. At the end of the long journey it appears that the prince is the djinni and the djinni is the prince. (The thirty birds are the same *simorgh* birds. The prince and the djinni externally contradict each other but are internally one. Thus the poet must discover a djinni or a hidden world, which is deep inside him.)

3. The East/orient, as far as Rimbaud was concerned, was as much a geographical entity as a concept or view; it was a horizon as much as a vertical dimension. Facing towards the orient and striving to reach it were, as we have seen, two of the most significant driving forces behind his poems. This was confirmed by the course of his life, which demonstrated that the orient wasn't just a dream or a wish but something that he needed, so he went to it. Was this why he stopped writing poetry? Did he go there after he stopped writing so that he could physically live what he had dreamed of and written about in his poetry? Or did he stop writing through language because of another preoccupation – writing through action? This was one of the basic tenets of Sufism, which favoured practice over writing, as if deliverance, if there was deliverance, could be achieved only through practice. Thus he set out to explore the world, not through the alchemy of language (in the West) but through the alchemy of work (in the East). It was as if he wanted, like the Sufi, to diminish the space between him and the imagined, so he emerged from descriptive language and went beyond the illusion that the words created, since, like the Sufi, he wanted his body to become the locus of transformation. He became one with existence in its entirety, instead of partially through his imagination.

# Selected Writings on Surrealism

## Books

Abastado, Claude, *Introduction au surréalisme*, Paris: Bordas, 1971.

—, *Le surréalisme*, Faire le point, Paris: Hachette, 1975.

—, 'Ecriture automatique et instance du sujet', *Revue des sciences humaines* [Lille], vol. 4, 1981, pp. 59–75.

Alexandrian, Sarane, *André Breton par lui-mème*, Paris: Le Seuil, 1971.

—, *Le surréalisme et le rêve*, Connaissance de l'inconscient, Paris: Gallimard, 1974.

—, *Les libérateurs de l'amour*, Paris: Le Seuil, 1977.

Alquié, Ferdinand, *Philosophie du surréalisme*, Paris: Flammarion, 1955.

—, 'Le surréalisme et l'art', *Les études philosophiques*, no. 2, 1975.

Anzieu, Didier, *L'auto-analyse de Freud et la découverte de la psychanalyse*, Paris: P.U.F., 1976.

Audoin, Philippe, *Breton*, Pour une bibliothèque idéale, Paris: Gallimard, 1970.

—, *Les Surréalistes*, Ecrivains de toujours, Paris: Le Seuil, 1973.

Bataille, Georges, 'La vieille taupe et le prefix "sur" dans les mots "surhomme" et "surréaliste"', *Oeuvres complètes*, vol. 2, Paris: Gallimard, 1970, pp. 93–109.

—, 'Le surréalisme au jour le jour', *Oeuvres complètes*, vol. 8, Paris: Gallimard, 1976, pp. 167–84.

Bedouin, Jean-Louis, *Vingt ans de surréalisme 1939–1959*, Paris: Denoël, 1969.

Benayoun, Robert, *Erotique du surréalisme*, Paris: Pauvert, 1965, 1978.

Benjamin, Walter, 'Le surréalisme: Le dernier instantané de l'intelligence européenne' [1929], in *Mythe et violence*, Paris: Les lettres nouvelles, 1971.

Blanchot, Maurice, *Le part du feu*, Paris: Gallimard, 1949.

—, *L'espace littéraire*, Paris: Gallimard, 1955.

Brechon, Robert, *Le surréalisme*, U2, Paris: Armand Cohn, 1971.

Caillois, Roger, *Approches de l'imaginaire*, Paris: Gallimard, 1974.

Camus, Albert, *L'homme révolté* [1951], Idées, Paris: Gallimard, 1963.

Carrouges, Michel, *André Breton et les données fondamentales du surréalisme* [1950], Idées, Paris: Gallimard, 1971.

—, *Les Machines célibataires*, revised edn, Paris: Le Chêne, 1976.

Daumal, René, 'Lettre ouverte à André Breton sur les rapports du surréalisme et du Grand Jeu', *Le Grand Jeu*, no. 3, autumn 1930, pp. 76–83.

Decottignies, Jean, 'L'oeuvre surréaliste et l'idéologie', *Littérature*, no. 1, February 1971, pp. 30–47.

Dupuis, J. F., *Histoire désinvolte du surréalisme*, Paris: Paul Vermont, 1977.

Durozol, Gerard, and Lecherbonnier, Bernard, *Le surréalisme: théories, thèmes, techniques*, Paris: Larousse, 1971.

Eigeldinger, Marc, *André Breton: Essais et témoignage*, Neuchâtel: La Baconnière, 1970.

—, 'Poésie et langage alchimique chez André Breton', *Mélusine*, no. 2, 1981.

—, 'Entretiens sur le surréalisme', *Le surréalisme et son influence sur la pensée, la poésie et l'art contemporains*, ed. Ferdinand Alquié, colloquium, Cerisy, 9–19 July 1966, Paris: Mouton, 1968.

Gauthier, Xavière, *Surréalisme et sexualité*, Idées, Paris: Gallimard, 1971.

Houdebine, Jean-Louis, 'Méconnaissance de la psychanalyse dans le discours surréaliste', *Tel quel*, no. 46, 1971.

Janover, Louis, *Surréalisme, art et politique,* Paris: Galilée, 1980.

Jouffroy, Alain, 'Quel est le critère de la surréalité? Le modèle intérieur', *xxe siècle*, no. 42, 1974.

—, *Le surréalisme*, Paris: Editions du xxe siècle, 1975.

Legoutie, Edmond, *Le Surréalisme*, Ensembles littéraires, Paris: Masson, 1972.

Legrand, Gerard, *André Breton en son temps*, Paris: Le Soleil Noir, 1976.

Masson, André, *Le rebelle du surréalisme Ecrits*, Paris: Hermann, 1976

Monnerot, Jules-Marcel, *La poésie moderne et le sacré*, Paris: Gallimard, 1945.

Nadeau, Maurice, *Histoire du surréalisme* [1945], Points, Paris: Le Seuil, 1972.

—, *Histoire du surréalisme: Documents surréalistes*, Paris: Le Seuil, 1948.

Passeron, René, *Encyclopédie du surréalisme*, Paris: Somogy, 1975.

Pierre, José, *Le surréalisme*, Lausanne: Editions Rencontre, 1966.

—, *Tracts surréalistes*, Paris: Losfeld, 1980–82.

Raymond, Marcel, *De Baudelaire au surréalisme*, Paris: José Corti, 1940.

Raymond de Reneville, André, 'Dernier état de la poésie surréaliste', *La N.R.F.*, February 1931.

—, *L'expérience poétique*, Paris: Gallimard, 1938, 1968.

Sartre, Jean-Paul, 'Qu'est-ce que la littérature?', in *Situation*, Paris: Gallimard, 1947.

Scarpetta, Guy, 'Limite-frontière du surréalisme', *Tel quel*, no. 46, summer 1971.

Starobinski, Jean, *La relation critique*, Paris: Gallimard, 1970.

Tison-Braun, Micheline, *Dada et le surrealism: textes théoriques sur la poésie*, Paris: Bordas, 1973.

## Periodicals

*Change 7°*, special edition on Surrealism, 1970.

'Le surréalisme', *Europe*, nos 475–6, November–December 1968.

*Mélusine,* Cahiers du Centre de recherches sur le surréalisme, Lausanne: Editions L'Age d'Homme, nos 1–5, 1978–84.

'André Breton et le mouvement surréaliste', *La N.R.F.*, no. 172, 1 April 1967.

'La Femme surréaliste', *Obliques*, vols 14–15, no. 4, 1977.

'Surréalisme international', *Opus international,* nos 19–20, October 1970.

*Tel quel,* no. 46, summer 1971.

# Index

## ALSO BY ADONIS

### An Introduction to Arab Poetics

Poetry is the quintessence of Arab culture. In this book, one of the foremost Arab poets reinterprets a rich and ancient heritage.

He examines the oral tradition of pre-Islamic Arabian poetry, as well as the relationship between Arabic poetry and the Qur'an, and between poetry and thought. Adonis also assesses the challenges of modernism and the impact of western culture on the Arab poetic tradition.

Stimulating in their originality, eloquent in their treatment of a wide range of poetry and criticism, these reflections open up fresh perspectives on one of the world's greatest – and least explored – literatures.

'The most intellectually stimulating of several Arab books of unique literary distinction in fine translations ... As important a cultural manifesto as any written today.'
Edward Said, *Independent on Sunday*

'The Arab world's greatest living poet has cultivated a garden of language.' *New York Times*

'Introduces the reader to a new way of interpreting all poetry, and to many marvellous words that do not have an English equivalent.' *Arts Letter*

Literary Criticism/Poetry • 978 0 86356 331 7 • £6.99

## ALSO BY ADONIS

### Victims of a Map
A Bilingual Anthology of Arabic Poetry

MAHMUD DARWISH, SAMIH AL-QASIM AND ADONIS

Mahmud Darwish, Samih al-Qasim and Adonis are amongst the leading poets in the Arab world today.

*Victims of a Map* presents some of their finest work in translation, alongside the original Arabic, including thirteen poems by Darwish never before published – in English or Arabic – and a long work by Adonis written during the 1982 siege of Beirut, also published here for the first time.

'A five-star publication … I would like to see it widely bought, read, and discussed in the English-speaking world.' *Orbis*

'A beautifully produced little book' *Middle East International*

'A very useful introduction to modern Arabic poetry … an elegant, precise translation.' *Al-Majalla*

'An excellent collection of verses from three of the most modern Arab poets.' *International Journal of Islamic and Arabic Studies*

Language/Literature • 978 0 86356 524 3 • £9.99